THE

MASTERING THE PUBLIC COMPANY

HOT

GENERAL COUNSEL ROLE

SEAT

CHAKA M. PATTERSON

StoryTerrace

To Mom,
who taught me that character matters more than applause
and that perseverance outlasts doubt.

To Tracey,
my partner in every sense of the word—your belief in me
has been the quiet force behind every page.

To Taylor and Chani,
you are my greatest inspiration and my proudest accomplishment.
Everything I build, I build with you in mind.

And to Myrtle Avenue,
where the foundation was laid.

This book carries my name, but it stands on your love.

✦

"The hot seat does not create leaders. It reveals who has done the work
long before the spotlight turns on."
— Chaka Patterson

Foreword

Chaka's *The Hot Seat* is the playbook both current and aspiring general counsels have been waiting to be written. I had the sincere pleasure of crossing paths with Chaka shortly after becoming General Counsel for NiSource Inc., a publicly traded utility company. His willingness to share and leverage his own experience in the general counsel's seat for the benefit of his future clients stands out as a differentiator. Chaka is a legal advisor but also a teacher and coach who understands important aspects of business—from the front lines to the boardroom, from department budgets to the company's balance sheet, to quarterly and annual earnings reports.

The only people who know what this seat is like are the ones who have held it. There are few comparators for navigating relationships, executive dynamics, and a board of directors while also addressing real-time, sensitive issues and maintaining the trust of an organization and its stakeholders. Someone who's sat in the seat knows, and that is what Chaka offers us in his new book. Chaka discusses the general counsel's many hats—risk manager, cultural beacon, and the organization's conscience. This is 100% consistent with the charge and advice that two of my greatest mentors (both prior and acting GCs) shared with me as I assumed the role. It's a tall order of responsibility, and it's not for everyone. How do you know if it's for you? If presented with the opportunity to serve in the role, where is your operating manual?

Chaka's *The Hot Seat* is an excellent guide. Having the opportunity to serve as general counsel is a privilege, but, as with anything, it is not without its burdens. Chaka superbly documents the responsibilities of the general counsel, as well as the characteristics and competencies that lead to success and keep us at the table.

Kim Cuccia
Executive Vice President, General Counsel, and Corporate Secretary
for NiSource Inc.

Contents

Introduction

My phone lit up at 8:31 a.m.—General Counsel—ACME. Right on schedule for the day to go sideways.

ACME is a $2 billion public company (NYSE: ACME) operating in the commercial-industrial space, and the GC is one of my coaching clients. For her to be calling this early, it must be urgent. So, I picked up on the first ring.

"What happened?"

"The stock is down twenty percent," she said. "At the open."

"Twenty?" I repeated.

"Yes." Her voice tightened. "And still falling."

In the background, I heard the telltale noise of crisis: papers shuffling, keyboards clacking, voices moving fast and too loud. She wasn't in her office. She was in the war room—the place companies go when they've suddenly remembered they can bleed.

"What triggered it?"

"We performed routine maintenance," she said, choosing each word like it might explode if handled carelessly. "On one component of a commercial product."

Okay, I thought. Maintenance happens. Components fail. You investigate, you fix, and you disclose if needed. Ugly, but survivable.

Then she said, "And the product failed. Spectacularly."

"Define spectacularly."

She exhaled—short and controlled. "There were people in it."

Silence. Not the awkward kind. The kind that drains a room of oxygen.

"How many?" I asked.

"Several hundred," she said quietly. "Lives potentially at risk. Maybe worse."

My grip tightened on the receiver.

Finally, as if she hadn't already dropped a piano on the conversation, she added, "And there's a research note out."

"A research note?" I asked, buying time.

"An investment bank analyst published a piece blaming the failure on our maintenance. It hit the street before we could even understand what we were dealing with."

I could picture it perfectly: clean fonts, confident conclusions, cautious language that still read like a verdict. The kind of report that moves markets and convinces people they've just witnessed the truth.

"Is he right?"

"No!" she said instantly. Too fast. Too certain. Almost desperate. The words should have been a relief. A life preserver. Instead, they landed like another weight because in the market, truth doesn't always win the first round. Sometimes it doesn't even make it into the ring.

"The report is wrong," she said again, now more to herself than to me.

I glanced at my computer screen, but I already knew what was happening: red arrows, sell orders, trading desks waking up to blood in the water as value evaporated by the second. The stock was still collapsing.

"The board is concerned," she said. "The CEO is angry. The CFO is angry. Everyone's angry."

Her voice sharpened—not with tears, but with something more dangerous: fear dressed up as control. "If we don't move, this company could be finished before lunch."

Then came the part she didn't have to say out loud, because I heard it anyway. Everyone was looking at her to fix this, and she had no idea where to start. I glanced down at the neat line I'd drawn across the top of my legal pad. Like I was about to take notes on an ordinary Tuesday. It wasn't going to be that kind of day.

The problem wasn't only the stock drop. Or the analyst. Or even the failure that had put hundreds of lives in jeopardy. The problem was simpler—and worse. When the world decides you're guilty, you don't get weeks or months to prove you're innocent. You get minutes. At 8:33 a.m., with the General Counsel waiting on the line, the countdown had already started . . . and there's only one question that matters.

What would you do?

What would you say to the CEO and CFO in the first five minutes? The only minutes that really count.

What would you tell the board?

What would you do about the analyst note?

What disclosures do you need—and when?

Whom do you call first: outside counsel, auditors, PR, regulators, or your insurer?

How do you keep the company from making the situation worse while everyone else is demanding immediate action?

And here's the hardest part. How do you make the right calls when you're exhausted, under attack, and missing half the facts?

That's the hot seat.

This book is about mastering it. It's a field guide for how to think, communicate, and lead like the strategic executive you are. Think of it as the practical MBA for lawyers at the top of their game.

We're going to talk about what actually works: the strategies, instincts, and habits that separate the GCs who survive from the ones who burn out, get sidelined, or quietly disappear after "a mutual decision" to pursue other opportunities. And we're going to do it the way the job happens: in real time, with imperfect information, competing stakeholders, and no luxury of clean decisions. I'll even share the advice I gave the Acme GC that made her the hero.

So, let's get started.

ONE

WELCOME TO THE HOT SEAT

—

NOW WHAT?

Welcome to the Hot Seat– Now What?

Congratulations. You've landed one of the most challenging, high-stakes legal jobs in corporate America. You're now the General Counsel (GC) of a public company—the legal guardian, risk manager, corporate diplomat, and, occasionally, the last sane person in the boardroom.

Here's what you might think your job is.

Ensuring the company follows the law.
Reviewing contracts, SEC filings, and policies.
Managing litigation and regulatory compliance.
Advising executives and the Board.

Sounds simple, right? Wrong.

The reality of the role is far more complex and multifaceted than many anticipate. If you've ever sat in the General Counsel chair of a public company—or even brushed up against it—you know the scenario described in the Introduction isn't hypothetical. It's inevitable. Maybe it's a crisis like that. Maybe it's a surprise subpoena. Maybe it's an activist investor who thinks your CEO is overpaid and your board is asleep. Maybe it's an

SEC comment letter that turns into something much worse. Maybe it's a whistleblower complaint that lands at the worst possible time. Or maybe it's just an ordinary Tuesday that suddenly becomes "the day" your company will talk about for the next decade.

No matter the trigger, the pattern is always the same:
- the pressure hits fast
- the room gets crowded
- everyone wants answers

and somehow, even when the issue isn't "legal," it becomes your problem.

Your CEO wants speed but demands perfection. They expect you to be a business partner (but also to make sure the company doesn't get into trouble with the government or get sued). The CFO wants you to be cost-conscious (but wants certainty, while believing in probabilities). The CHRO wants partnerships but carries cultural landmines. The Board wants clear guidance. (But they also want to avoid liability, so they might ask for "creative" solutions.) They hate surprises. The SEC has a long memory and a short fuse. And investors? They don't care about your legal headaches—just the stock price.

Oh, and by the way, you'll be on call 24/7. Your phone will buzz during family dinners, board meetings will stretch into the late hours, and the pressure to keep everything above board will be constant. The National Association of Corporate Directors even declares that you are now the first and last line of defense against legal, ethical, and reputational calamities.[1]

Still excited? You should be. This is one of the most rewarding and influential jobs in the corporate world, but only if you know how to navigate it. The unique blend of legal expertise, business acumen, and interpersonal skills required makes it both demanding and deeply fulfilling. The decisions you make can shape the future of the company, protect its stakeholders, and uphold the integrity of the market.

Let's get you up to speed.

---

1 NACD Blue Ribbon Commission Report on the Evolving Role of the GC, 2021. https://www.nacdonline.org/all-governance/governance-resources/governance-research/outlook-and-challenges/2021-governance-outlook-projections-on-emerging-board-matters/

Here's what your job actually is.

Anticipating Risk Before It Becomes a Lawsuit, SEC probe, or PR Nightmare.

This involves staying ahead of industry trends, regulatory changes, and potential vulnerabilities within the company. It means proactively identifying risks that may not be immediately obvious and developing strategies to mitigate them.

Managing People and Politics:
Because Legal Advice is Worthless if No One Listens to It.

This is about building trust and credibility with key stakeholders, understanding their perspectives and motivations, and communicating legal advice in a way that resonates with them. It also means navigating internal power dynamics and influencing decision-making processes.

Making Judgment Calls with Incomplete Information.

You'll rarely have all the facts, but you'll still have to decide. In the fast-paced world of a public company, decisions often need to be made quickly, with limited information. The GC must be able to assess risks and benefits, weigh competing interests, and exercise sound judgment in the face of uncertainty.

Balancing Business Needs with Legal Risks.

The company wants to move fast; your job is to make sure it doesn't trip over itself. This is about finding creative solutions that allow the company to achieve its business objectives while minimizing legal risks. It requires a deep understanding of the company's business, its strategic goals, and the legal and regulatory landscape in which it operates.

Playing Corporate Firefighter.

When something goes wrong (and it will), everyone will turn to you. Whether it's a data breach, a product recall, or a whistleblower complaint, the GC is often the first person called when a crisis erupts. They must be able to quickly assess the situation, develop a response strategy, and manage communications with internal and external stakeholders.

Being a Proactive Educator.
You are responsible for ensuring that all employees, from the C-suite to entry-level positions, understand the company's ethical and legal obligations. This involves creating and delivering training programs, developing clear and concise policies, and fostering a culture of compliance throughout the organization.

Understanding the Interplay of Global Regulations.
In an increasingly interconnected world, public companies often operate across multiple jurisdictions, each with its own unique set of laws and regulations. The GC must have a strong understanding of international law and be able to navigate the complexities of cross-border transactions and regulatory compliance.

Staying Abreast of Technological Advancements.
Emerging technologies such as artificial intelligence, blockchain, and cybersecurity pose new legal and ethical challenges for public companies. The GC must stay informed about these developments and advise the company on how to mitigate the associated risks.

In short, you're not just a lawyer; you're a business executive, strategist, risk manager, educator, and global citizen. You are the conscience of the company, the gladiator/protector of its reputation, and the guardian of its long-term sustainability.

The Three Hard Truths Every Public Company GC Must Accept

The role of a public company GC is not always glamorous or easy. There are certain hard truths that every GC must accept to be successful.

1. You Will Have to Make Uncomfortable Calls

You'll face situations with no easy answers. Sometimes, you'll have to tell the CEO or board what they don't want to hear.

- There will be times when your advice contradicts the CEO's vision, investor pressure, or market expectations.
- You must be prepared to say "no" to risky decisions, even if it means conflict with leadership.
- Protecting the company sometimes means making choices that are unpopular but legally necessary.

Strategy for Navigating this Situation

Develop a Strong Ethical Compass. Base your decisions on a clear set of ethical principles.

Be Prepared to Defend Your Position. Back up your advice with solid legal reasoning and business data.

Document Everything. Keep a record of all your advice and the rationale behind it.

Seek Support from Outside Counsel. If you are facing a particularly difficult decision, seek advice from outside counsel.

Be Willing to Resign. If you are asked to do something that you believe is illegal or unethical, be willing to resign.

2. The Best Legal Advice Won't Matter if No One Listens

Your influence depends on how well you communicate and build relationships.

- If people trust you, they'll listen. If they don't, you're just another lawyer in the room.
- Legal expertise alone isn't enough—you must be a persuasive communicator.
- Building relationships and trust with executives and board members ensures your voice is heard.
- Without buy-in from leadership, even the best legal strategies will be ineffective.

Strategy for Navigating this Situation

Develop Your Communication Skills. Learn how to communicate legal advice in a clear, concise, and persuasive manner.

Build Relationships. Take the time to get to know the key stakeholders in the company and build relationships based on trust and mutual respect.

Be a Good Listener. Listen to the concerns of others and try to understand their perspectives.

Be a Problem Solver. Focus on finding solutions that meet the needs of all stakeholders.

Be a Team Player. Work collaboratively with others to achieve the company's goals.

3. This Job is a Marathon, not a Sprint

The GC role is relentless—but don't burn yourself out.

- Know when to step back, delegate, and manage expectations.
- The relentless nature of the GC role requires stamina, resilience, and balance.
- Prioritizing mental health, delegation, and work-life boundaries is crucial to long-term success.
- Learning to manage expectations and push back, when necessary, will help you sustain your effectiveness in the role.

Strategy for Navigating this Situation

Prioritize Your Mental Health. Make time for activities that help you relax and de-stress.

Delegate Effectively. Delegate tasks to your team members and trust them to get the job done.

Manage Expectations. Be realistic about what you can accomplish and don't be afraid to say "no."

Set Boundaries. Establish clear boundaries between your work and personal life.

Take Vacations. Take regular vacations to recharge and refresh.

More Than Just Legal Eagle: The GC as the Conscience of the Company

In addition to being the company's chief legal officer—a role demanding expertise in corporate law, risk management, and regulatory compliance—you are now also expected to be its moral compass. This expectation isn't explicitly written in your job description, nor is it likely to be a topic broached during your initial interviews. However, whether you wanted it or not, the role of GC comes with an unspoken expectation: ensuring the company does what's right, and not just what's legal. This expectation stems from the GC's unique position within the organization.

The GC sits at the intersection of law, business strategy, and public perception. They have a bird's-eye view of all company operations, understand the legal ramifications of business decisions, and are often the first to identify potential ethical lapses. This places them in a crucial position to influence corporate behavior and champion ethical conduct.

The concept of the GC as the "conscience of the company" might sound lofty, but it's grounded in practicality. In today's hyper-connected world, a company's ethical reputation is as valuable as its brand. Ethical lapses can lead to devastating consequences, including legal penalties, financial losses, reputational damage, and a loss of trust from stakeholders. Therefore, the GC's role in guiding the company toward ethical decision-making is essential for long-term sustainability and success.

This responsibility involves more than just interpreting laws and regulations; it requires a deep understanding of the company's values, a commitment to ethical principles, and the courage to speak up when ethical concerns arise. The GC must be a trusted advisor to the CEO and the board, providing guidance on ethical dilemmas and ensuring that decisions are made with integrity.

Personal Development and Skills Enhancement for a Public Company GC

To thrive in the role of a public company GC, continuous learning and development are essential.

Executive Education Programs. Consider programs focused on leadership, strategy, and finance to broaden your business acumen.

Legal Conferences and Seminars. Attend industry-specific legal conferences to stay updated on the latest legal trends and network with peers.

Mentorship. Seek out a mentor who is an experienced GC or business leader to provide guidance and support.

Networking. Build a strong network of legal and business professionals to exchange ideas and best practices.

Technology Training. Stay abreast of emerging technologies and their legal implications through specialized training programs.

The Evolving Legal Landscape and Emerging Challenges

The legal and regulatory landscape is constantly evolving, presenting new challenges for public company GCs.

Cybersecurity and Data Privacy. Develop robust cybersecurity policies and procedures to protect company data and comply with data privacy regulations like GDPR and CCPA.

Artificial Intelligence (AI). Understand the legal and ethical implications of AI and develop policies to ensure responsible use of AI technologies.

Supply Chain Risks. Assess and mitigate legal and ethical risks in the company's supply chain.

Geopolitical Risks. Monitor geopolitical developments and their potential impact on the company's operations.

Final Thought: Welcome to the Club

Being a public company GC is not for the faint of heart—but it's one of the most impactful, high-stakes jobs in corporate law. It demands a unique blend of legal expertise, business acumen, and interpersonal skills. The decisions you make can shape the future of the company, protect its stakeholders, and uphold the integrity of the market.

This book will give you the tools, strategies, and insights to thrive. By understanding the complexities of the role, building strong relationships with key stakeholders, and staying ahead of the curve on emerging legal and regulatory challenges, you can excel as a public company GC.

So, let's get to work.

TWO

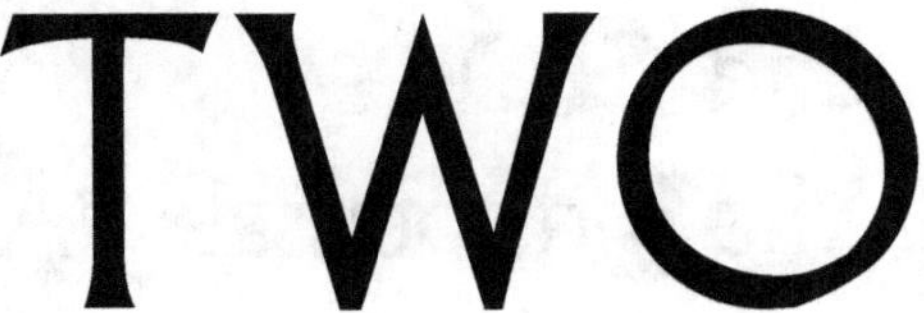

THE CEO AND CFO

—

BECOMING THE INDISPENSABLE ADVISOR

The CEO and CFO— Becoming the Indispensable Advisor

As General Counsel, your role transcends the traditional boundaries of legal risk management. You are a strategic advisor, a business partner, and a critical link between the company's vision and its legal obligations. Becoming the indispensable advisor, particularly to the CEO and CFO, is not merely a political game; it's about establishing influence, building trust, and ensuring the company's long-term success and ethical standing.

The CEO and CFO, while sharing the common goal of company prosperity, often operate from distinct perspectives. The CEO, the visionary leader, is driven by growth, innovation, and market dominance. Their focus is on seizing opportunities, expanding horizons, and achieving ambitious goals. This forward-thinking mindset can sometimes lead to a desire to "push the envelope," testing the limits of legal boundaries in pursuit of competitive advantage.

The CFO, on the other hand, is the pragmatic guardian of the company's financial health. They are laser-focused on profitability, cost control, and risk mitigation. Their analytical approach and deep understanding of financial statements make them acutely aware of potential liabilities and the financial impact of legal missteps. They may view Legal as a cost center, scrutinizing budgets and demanding efficiency.

Your challenge as General Counsel is to bridge this gap and to serve as a trusted advisor to both the CEO and CFO while upholding the highest ethical and legal standards. This requires a delicate balancing act: supporting the CEO's vision while safeguarding the company from legal risks and collaborating with the CFO to manage legal costs effectively while ensuring adequate protection.

Understanding Their Worlds: Empathy as a Strategic Tool

The CEO's Perspective

Strategic Vision. CEOs are responsible for defining the company's long-term direction. They are constantly scanning the horizon for opportunities—new markets, acquisitions, partnerships, and innovations that can propel the organization forward.

Market Competition. CEOs operate in a high-stakes environment where agility and bold moves can mean the difference between market leadership and obsolescence.

Investor Expectations. They are under relentless pressure from shareholders and the board to deliver growth, profitability, and returns on investment.

Risk Appetite. CEOs often have a higher tolerance for risk, seeking to capitalize on opportunities before competitors do.

The CFO's Perspective

Financial Stewardship. CFOs ensure the company's financial health, focusing on cash flow, budgeting, and long-term sustainability.

Regulatory Compliance. They must ensure that all financial practices meet legal and regulatory standards—Sarbanes-Oxley, SEC requirements, tax codes, etc.

Risk Management. CFOs are tasked with identifying, quantifying, and mitigating financial risks, often favoring conservative approaches.

Cost Control. They scrutinize expenditures, including legal costs, to maximize value and minimize waste.

The GC's Strategic Role: More Than Legal Advice

1. Translator & Bridge-Builder

Translating Vision into Compliance. The GC helps the CEO understand the legal implications of strategic initiatives, identifying both opportunities and red flags early.

Bridging Risk Tolerances. The GC mediates between the CEO's appetite for risk and the CFO's focus on caution, proposing solutions that advance business goals while staying within legal and ethical boundaries.

2. Trusted Advisor & Ethical Guardian

Building Trust. By demonstrating empathy, the GC earns the trust of both executives, making it more likely that their advice will be sought and heeded in critical moments.

Upholding Integrity. The GC ensures that neither ambition nor caution leads the company astray, preventing legal shortcuts for the CEO and excessive risk aversion for the CFO.

3. Cost-Conscious Partner

Legal Budgeting. The GC works with the CFO to forecast and manage legal expenses, prioritizing matters that present the greatest risk or opportunity.

Efficiency Initiatives. They may introduce technology (e.g., contract automation, e-discovery tools) and process improvements to reduce costs without compromising legal protection.

Your challenge as General Counsel is to bridge this gap and to serve as a trusted advisor to both the CEO and CFO while upholding the highest ethical and legal standards. This requires a delicate balancing act: supporting the CEO's vision while safeguarding the company from legal risks and collaborating with the CFO to manage legal costs effectively while ensuring adequate protection. This is a strategic imperative, not a mere administrative function.

Key Takeaways
- A GC must see issues through the CEO's and CFO's eyes, anticipating their concerns and motivations.
- Strategic communication ensures both executives understand the value and rationale behind legal recommendations.
- Balanced solutions enable the company to pursue growth and innovation without sacrificing financial discipline or legal integrity.

The CEO: Your Toughest Client

The CEO's job is to drive growth, build shareholder value, and keep the board happy. Your job? Make sure they don't do something reckless in the process. This is a delicate balancing act, requiring you to be both a trusted advisor and a voice of caution.

How to Work With the CEO

Be a problem solver, not a roadblock. CEOs hate hearing "no." Your job is to say, "Here's how we can do this legally." Instead of simply pointing out the risks, offer alternative solutions that achieve the desired business outcome while mitigating potential legal issues.

Be practical. If your legal advice is too abstract, they'll ignore it. Keep it short, actionable, and tied to business goals. Frame your advice in terms of business impact, quantifying the potential risks and rewards in financial terms.

Educate them on legal risks proactively. Don't wait for a crisis to explain the importance of legal compliance. Schedule regular meetings to discuss emerging legal trends, regulatory changes, and potential vulnerabilities within the company.

Understand their vision. Take the time to understand the CEO's strategic goals and priorities. This will allow you to align your legal advice with their overall vision for the company.

Be a trusted confidant. The CEO needs to be able to trust you to provide candid and objective advice, even when it's not what they want to hear. Build a relationship based on honesty, integrity, and mutual respect.

Key Takeaways
- Build trust with the CEO by aligning legal strategies with business goals.
- Provide solutions instead of just identifying problems.
- Be proactive in risk management rather than reactive.
- Communicate legal advice in a clear, concise, and business-oriented manner.
- Be a trusted confidant and provide candid, objective advice.

The CFO: Your Partner (and Occasional Opponent)

The CFO controls the company's financial health—and your legal budget. Your interests align . . . until legal expenses come up. This relationship requires a delicate balance of collaboration and advocacy.

How to Work With the CFO

Speak their language. Understand financial statements, earnings reports, and key metrics. Demonstrate an understanding of the company's financial performance and how legal decisions impact the bottom line.

Show that Legal is a business enabler, not just a cost center. Quantify the value of legal services by highlighting how they prevent costly litigation, protect intellectual property, and ensure regulatory compliance.

Engage early in financial planning to align risk management with financial strategies. Participate in budget discussions and advocate for adequate resources to support legal compliance and risk mitigation efforts.

Be transparent about legal spending. Provide regular updates on legal expenses, explaining the rationale behind each expenditure and demonstrating a commitment to cost-effectiveness.

Find creative solutions to manage legal costs. Explore alternative billing arrangements, such as fixed fees or capped fees, to provide greater predictability and control over legal spend.

Key Takeaways
- Speak the CFO's language. Understand financial statements and key performance metrics.
- Demonstrate how legal compliance contributes to long-term financial stability.
- Advocate for legal budget needs with a business-minded approach. Be transparent about legal spend and demonstrate a commitment to cost-effectiveness.
- Find creative solutions to manage legal costs.

How to Be a Trusted Advisor: Moving Beyond "No" to Strategic Solutions

The traditional image of a lawyer as a compliance cop, simply pointing out what cannot be done, is no longer sufficient. Today's CEOs seek legal partners who understand their business objectives, anticipate challenges, and offer creative solutions. Falling into the trap of becoming a "yes man"—rubber-stamping decisions to maintain favor'—is equally detrimental. It undermines your credibility and ultimately puts the company at risk.

The Essence of Trusted Advice
Proactive Engagement. Trusted advisors are not brought in as an afterthought. They are involved early in the decision-making process, providing guidance and shaping strategy from the outset. This means attending key meetings, participating in strategic planning sessions, and proactively identifying potential legal issues.

Understanding the Business. To provide meaningful advice, you must have a deep understanding of the company's industry, its competitive landscape, its financial performance, and its strategic goals. This requires ongoing learning, research, and engagement with various departments within the organization.

Translating Legal Concepts. Legal jargon is a barrier to effective communication. Translate complex legal concepts into clear, concise language that resonates with the CEO and CFO, focusing on the business implications of legal issues. Use analogies, examples, and visual aids to illustrate your points.

Offering Solutions, Not Just Problems. When pointing out a legal risk, always offer alternative approaches or mitigation strategies. Demonstrate that you are not simply a roadblock, but a problem-solver. Present a range of options, with clear explanations of the risks and benefits of each.

Building Relationships. Cultivate strong relationships with the CEO and CFO, built on mutual respect, open communication, and a shared commitment to the company's success. This requires regular communication, active listening, and a genuine interest in their perspectives.

Building Credibility: A Multifaceted Approach

Demonstrate Business Acumen. Go beyond legal expertise and show a strong understanding of the company's financial statements, market trends, and competitive dynamics. Attend industry conferences, read business publications, and seek opportunities to learn about the company's operations.

Be Proactive. Anticipate legal issues before they arise and proactively develop solutions. Conduct regular legal risk assessments, monitor regulatory changes, and develop compliance programs to prevent legal problems.

Communicate Effectively. Tailor your communication style to the CEO and CFO, using clear, concise language and focusing on the business implications of legal advice. Avoid legal jargon and present your advice in a way that is actionable and easy to understand.

Be Responsive. Respond promptly to inquiries and provide timely updates on legal matters. Set clear expectations for response times and consistently meet or exceed those expectations.

Be a Team Player. Collaborate with other departments and build strong working relationships across the organization. Attend cross-functional meetings, participate in company events, and be willing to help other departments with their legal needs.

Embrace Technology. Utilize technology to streamline legal processes, improve efficiency, and enhance communication. Implement legal project management software, contract management systems, and e-discovery tools.

Navigating the CEO's "Envelope-Pushing": Strategies for Responsible Guidance

CEOs are inherently risk-takers, driven by a desire to innovate, disrupt, and achieve ambitious goals. This can sometimes lead to situations where they want to push the boundaries of legal and ethical norms. As General Counsel, your role is not to stifle their ambition, but to guide them towards responsible decision-making that protects the company's interests.

Strategies for Pushing Back on the CEO

1. **The 'Red Light, Yellow Light, Green Light' Approach**
   Red Light. High-risk activities that are clearly illegal or unethical. Examples include fraudulent accounting practices, insider trading, or violations of environmental regulations. **Example:** A CEO proposes backdating stock options to attract and retain talent. This is a clear Red-Light issue with severe legal and reputational consequences.
   Yellow Light. Activities with potential legal risks that can be managed through mitigation strategies. Examples include aggressive marketing claims, data privacy concerns, or potential antitrust issues. **Example:** A CEO wants to launch a new advertising campaign that makes comparative claims about competitors' products. This is a Yellow Light issue that requires careful substantiation and compliance with advertising regulations.
   Green Light. Activities that are legally sound and align with ethical standards. These should be encouraged and supported. **Example:** A CEO wants to implement a new employee wellness program that

promotes healthy lifestyles. This is a Green Light issue that can improve employee morale and productivity.

2. Data-Driven Decision Making: Beyond Gut Feelings

Instead of relying solely on legal opinions, present data-driven insights to support your recommendations. This could include:

Case law precedents. Provide specific examples of similar cases and their outcomes.

Regulatory enforcement actions. Highlight recent enforcement actions by regulatory agencies and the penalties imposed.

Industry benchmarks. Compare the company's legal risk profile to industry peers.

Financial risk assessments. Quantify the potential financial impact of legal risks.

Example: "CEO, while I understand the desire to recognize revenue this quarter for a big sale, in 2018, the SEC fined ABC company $10 million for premature revenue recognition, and our auditors have told us that there is a high likelihood that the SEC would investigate us for that kind of recognition."

3. Enlisting Allies: Building a Coalition of Reason

When faced with a CEO who is resistant to legal advice, strategically involve other key stakeholders.

CFO. Frame the legal risks in financial terms to gain their support. **Example:** "CFO, if we don't fully comply with these consumer protection regulations, we could face fines upwards of $500,000 per violation, significantly impacting our bottom line."

Board Members. Present the legal implications of the CEO's proposed actions to the board for their guidance. **Example:** "Board members, the CEO is proposing a new market strategy that would involve entering into a nation without any IP protection for our key patents. I'm flagging for you that doing so would open us up to significant IP theft."

External Counsel. Obtain an independent legal opinion from a reputable law firm to reinforce your advice. **Example:** "We've engaged with external counsel to give a second opinion on the permissibility of this new strategy. They are also of the opinion that it is too risky because of the high probability of regulatory fines."

4. Documentation: Protecting Yourself and the Company
Maintain a detailed record of your legal advice, including:
- the CEO's proposed actions
- the legal risks involved
- your recommendations
- the CEO's decision
- any dissenting opinions

This documentation can protect you from personal liability and provide a clear record of the decision-making process.

Example: After a meeting, send a follow-up email summarizing your understanding of the decisions made and reiterating your legal advice. Store all relevant documents in a secure and accessible location.

Strategies for Influencing the CEO

"What If" Scenarios. Present hypothetical scenarios to illustrate the potential consequences of the CEO's proposed actions. **Example:** "What if a competitor sues us for patent infringement based on this new product design? What would be the potential costs of litigation, damages, and reputational harm?"

Ethical Frameworks. Introduce ethical frameworks, such as utilitarianism or deontology, to guide the CEO's decision-making process. **Example:** "From a utilitarian perspective, would this action maximize overall benefit to all stakeholders, or would it primarily benefit shareholders at the expense of employees, customers, or the environment?"

Reputational Risk Assessments. Quantify the potential reputational damage that could result from the CEO's actions. **Example:** "A negative news article about this issue could damage our brand reputation, leading to a decline in sales, customer loyalty, and investor confidence."

Long-Term Value Focus. Emphasize the importance of long-term value creation over short-term gains. **Example:** "While this action may provide a short-term boost to our stock price, it could ultimately harm our long-term sustainability and competitiveness."

Understanding Behavioral Economics

CEOs, like all individuals, are subject to cognitive biases that can influence their decision-making. Understanding these biases can help you tailor your approach.

Key Biases Affecting CEOs

Confirmation Bias. This is the tendency to seek out or give more weight to information that confirms existing beliefs, while ignoring or dismissing evidence that contradicts them. In a business context, confirmation bias can lead CEOs to favor strategies or projects they already believe in, potentially overlooking critical risks or alternative opportunities. For example, a leader might only focus on positive market feedback for a new product while disregarding warning signs or continue investing in a failing project due to the "sunk cost fallacy."

Overconfidence Bias. Overconfidence leads individuals to overestimate their knowledge, abilities, or the accuracy of their judgments. For CEOs, this can manifest as underestimating risks, overcommitting resources, or ignoring dissenting opinions. High-profile corporate failures, such as Nokia's decline or Enron's collapse, have been linked to executive overconfidence, where leaders dismissed external threats or warnings due to an inflated sense of certainty. Overconfidence can also stifle open dialogue, making it harder for teams to challenge flawed assumptions.

Anchoring Bias. Anchoring bias is the tendency to rely too heavily on the first piece of information received (the "anchor") when making decisions. For CEOs, this might mean basing a strategic plan on early projections or initial market data, even when more comprehensive or updated information becomes available. Anchoring can skew risk assessments and lead to suboptimal choices if leaders do not actively seek out diverse perspectives and additional data.

Strategies for General Counsel to Address Executive Biases

1. Constructively Challenge Executive Decisions

The GC requests a meeting with the CEO and executive team to discuss the legal, reputational, and operational risks associated with the product. Instead of simply flagging risks, the GC frames their input within the broader business context: "While the early feedback is promising, there are significant privacy concerns that could expose us to regulatory fines and reputational damage. Here are alternative approaches to address these issues before launch." This positions the GC as a strategic partner, not just a gatekeeper.

2. Promote Deliberative and Structured Decision-Making

To counter overconfidence and anchoring, the GC advocates for a structured decision-making process. They introduce a decision matrix that requires the team to weigh all available data, including dissenting opinions and updated market research. The GC also suggests regular decision checkpoints and invites cross-functional leaders to contribute their perspectives, ensuring that the process is not driven solely by intuition or initial impressions.

3. Leverage Data and Objective Analysis

The GC requests an independent market analysis and legal review, presenting the findings in an objective, data-driven format. They encourage the CEO and team to consider not only supporting evidence but also data that contradicts their assumptions. For example, "Here's a benchmarking report showing how similar products faced regulatory hurdles in Europe. Let's discuss how we can proactively address these risks".

4. Facilitate Diverse Perspectives and Open Dialogue

Recognizing the risk of groupthink, the GC champions a culture of open dialogue. They propose forming a "red team" tasked with challenging the product's go-to-market strategy and identifying blind spots. The GC ensures that meetings include time for dissenting voices and alternative scenarios, reinforcing psychological safety and cognitive diversity within the leadership team.

5. Routine Access and Escalation Protocols

The GC maintains regular access to the board and relevant committees, such as audit and risk. They brief the board on the potential biases, the product decision, and they outline the steps being taken to ensure objective, compliant, and ethical decision-making. If necessary, the GC is prepared to escalate concerns through established influencing protocols, reinforcing their duty to the organization and its stakeholders.

By systematically applying these strategies, the GC helps the CEO and executive team recognize and mitigate their biases. The company ultimately decides to delay the product launch, address privacy concerns, and pilot the device with a smaller user group. This approach reduces risk, improves stakeholder trust, and demonstrates the GC's value as both an ethical compass and a strategic business partner.

Partnering with the CFO: Beyond Cost Control—a Strategic Partnership

A high-functioning partnership between the General Counsel (GC) and Chief Financial Officer (CFO) is increasingly vital as organizations face rising legal complexity and budgetary pressures. Beyond traditional cost control, GCs can adopt a more strategic, value-driven approach to working with the CFO, strengthening both the legal function and the company's overall performance.

Strategic Alignment and Blueprinting

- Develop a shared strategic blueprint that aligns legal department objectives with broader organizational goals. This plan should address both operational efficiencies and risk management, integrating technological tools such as contract management systems and spend management software to streamline processes and provide actionable data for both legal and finance leaders.
- Regularly review and benchmark legal department performance against similar organizations to identify best practices and set realistic, mutually agreed-upon key performance indicators (KPIs) for legal spend and outcomes.

Enhanced Communication and Transparency

- Foster transparent, ongoing communication with the CFO. This includes not only sharing regular reports on legal spend and risk but also proactively discussing upcoming legal challenges and opportunities for collaboration.
- Utilize shared workspaces and collaborative tools to ensure both departments have real-time access to relevant data, facilitating faster, more informed decision-making.

Operational Efficiency and Scenario Planning

- Implement robust expense tracking and categorization systems to provide granular visibility into legal costs, enabling the identification of trends and areas for improvement.
- Work with the CFO to develop scenario-based budgets (best-case, worst-case, most likely) for legal spend, ensuring the organization is prepared for both routine and unexpected legal events.
- Establish clear budgetary expectations and performance metrics and communicate these across both teams to drive accountability and continuous improvement.

Risk Management and Quantification

- Collaborate on enterprise risk management frameworks that integrate both legal and financial perspectives, ensuring that all significant risks—whether regulatory, contractual, or operational—are identified, assessed, and prioritized for mitigation.

- Present legal risks in financial terms, using quantifiable metrics and visual tools such as heat maps to help the CFO understand the potential impact on the company's bottom line and allocate resources accordingly.

Leveraging Technology and Innovation

- Advocate for and implement legal technology solutions, such as e-discovery platforms, document automation, and enterprise legal management (ELM) systems that increase efficiency and provide measurable return-on-investment (ROI).
- Use legal dashboards to track and visualize key metrics (litigation costs, compliance rates, contract cycle times), making it easier for the CFO to monitor legal department performance and support data-driven budgeting.

Building a Culture of Collaboration

- Engage in regular cross-functional meetings and team-building activities to build trust and understanding between legal and finance teams.
- Encourage joint participation in major business initiatives, such as mergers, acquisitions, or regulatory compliance projects, to ensure both legal and financial considerations are integrated from the outset.

Demonstrating Value Beyond Compliance

- Proactively identify and communicate how legal initiatives contribute to revenue growth, cost savings, and risk reduction. For example, show how improved contract negotiation or intellectual property protection directly enhances the company's financial position.
- Conduct and present (ROI) analyses for major legal projects, helping the CFO see the tangible value of legal services in terms of avoided costs or increased asset value.

Five-Point Framework for Effective General Counsel Collaboration With The CEO and CFO

1. **Bridge Builder: Translate and Balance Business Vision with Legal and Financial Realities**
   - Serve as the translator between the CEO's growth-driven vision and the CFO's risk-averse, cost-focused approach.
   - Help the CEO understand the legal implications of strategic initiatives and frame legal requirements as enablers, not obstacles, to business goals.
   - Mediate between the CEO's appetite for risk and the CFO's emphasis on caution, proposing solutions that advance business objectives while staying within ethical and legal boundaries.

2. **Trusted Advisor: Build Credibility through Empathy, Integrity, and Proactive Engagement**
   - Develop deep empathy for both the CEO's and CFO's perspectives by understanding their unique pressures, motivations, and success metrics.
   - Earn trust by being involved early in decision-making, providing actionable advice and upholding ethical standards, even when it means constructively challenging executive decisions.
   - Move beyond simply saying "no" by offering creative, strategic alternatives and mitigation strategies, positioning yourself as a problem-solver, not a roadblock.

3. **Cost-Conscious Partner: Drive Legal Efficiency and Demonstrate Value**
   - Collaborate with the CFO to forecast, manage, and justify legal expenses, prioritizing resources for matters with the greatest risk or opportunity.
   - Implement technology and process improvements (e.g., contract automation, legal spend management, dashboards) to increase transparency, reduce costs, and improve efficiency without sacrificing legal protection.

- Establish benchmark legal operations against industry standards and communicate the ROI of legal initiatives in terms of CFO values-cost savings, risk reduction, and revenue enablement.

4. Strategic Influencer: Communicate Effectively and Counter Executive Biases

- Translate complex legal concepts into clear, concise language focused on business impact, using analogies, data, and visual aids.
- Leverage data-driven insights, case precedents, and financial quantification to support recommendations and influence executive decisions.
- Recognize and address cognitive biases (confirmation, overconfidence, anchoring) by promoting structured decision-making, encouraging diverse perspectives, and facilitating open dialogue.

5. Collaborative Leader: Foster Cross-Functional Alignment and a Culture of Partnership

- Build strong, regular communication channels with both the CEO and CFO, including joint meetings, shared digital workspaces, and scenario planning.
- Engage in cross-functional initiatives and team building to foster trust and understanding between legal, finance, and business units.
- Proactively demonstrate how Legal contributes to business growth, innovation, and risk management, making Legal an indispensable partner in achieving the company's long-term goals.

This framework synthesizes the chapter's practical guidance: The General Counsel's effectiveness hinges on empathy, proactive engagement, clear communication, strategic influence, and a collaborative, value-driven mindset that bridges the worlds of the CEO and CFO while safeguarding the company's integrity and success.

Case Studies

Scenario I: Mergers & Acquisitions (M&A)
The CEO is excited about acquiring a fast-growing startup to expand into a new market. The CFO is concerned about the acquisition's price, integration costs, and potential liabilities.

CEO's Perspective:
- sees the acquisition as a means for accelerating growth and beating competitors
- wants to move quickly before another company makes a bid
- focuses on potential synergies and market share gains

CFO's Perspective:
- worries about overpaying or hidden financial risks (e.g., undisclosed debts, pending lawsuits)
- concerned about the impact on the company's balance sheet and cash flow
- wants detailed due diligence and a clear financial plan for integration

Your Approach: With the CEO
- frame legal due diligence to "clear the runway" for a smooth acquisition, not as a roadblock
- highlight how legal structuring (e.g., indemnities, reps and warranties) can protect the company while enabling speed
- offer creative solutions for deal terms that balance risk and reward

Your Approach: With the CFO
- provide a clear, itemized risk assessment (e.g., pending litigation, IP ownership issues, compliance gaps)
- work with Finance to quantify potential exposures and mitigation strategies
- help negotiate deal terms that minimize financial risk (e.g., escrow arrangements, earn-outs)

The GC's approach ensures the CEO's growth ambitions are supported, while the CFO's need for risk mitigation and financial clarity is respected. The deal proceeds with appropriate safeguards and clear accountability.

Scenario II: Regulatory Crisis

A government agency launches an investigation into the company's business practices. The situation is urgent and could have serious legal, financial, and reputational consequences.

CEO's Perspective:

- focused on protecting the company's reputation and maintaining stakeholder trust
- wants to resolve the issue quickly to avoid business disruption
- concerned about media coverage and customer reactions

CFO's Perspective:

- focused on potential fines, penalties, and the cost of legal defense
- needs to assess the impact on financial statements and disclosures
- wants to ensure compliance with reporting requirements

Your Approach: With the CEO

- develop a crisis communication plan to address stakeholders and media, emphasizing transparency and responsibility
- advise on immediate steps to demonstrate cooperation and good faith to regulators
- frame legal actions as part of a broader strategy to restore trust and business continuity

Your Approach: With the CFO

- quantify potential financial exposures and work with Finance to set aside reserves if necessary
- coordinate with external auditors and ensure timely, accurate disclosures
- help manage legal costs by prioritizing actions and selecting the right outside counsel

The GC's leadership ensures a coordinated response that addresses both reputational and financial risks, preserving the company's credibility and stability.

Scenario III: Cost-Cutting Initiatives

The company is facing margin pressure and needs to reduce expenses. The CEO wants to free up resources for innovation, while the CFO is tasked with cutting overhead, including legal spend.

CEO's Perspective:

- Wants to ensure cost-cutting doesn't slow down strategic projects or innovation.
- Seeks to reallocate resources to high-growth areas

CFO's Perspective:

- Focused on achieving specific cost-reduction targets
- Wants clear justification for every dollar spent on legal services

Your Approach: With the CEO

- identify legal processes that can be streamlined or automated to support innovation (e.g., contract management tools)
- prioritize legal support for strategic initiatives, ensuring critical projects aren't delayed
- explain how efficient legal operations are a competitive advantage

Your Approach: With the CFO

- analyze legal spend and benchmarks against industry standards
- propose alternative fee arrangements with outside counsel (e.g., fixed fees, volume discounts)
- implement technology to track and report legal costs, providing transparency and accountability

The GC helps the company achieve its cost-reduction goals while maintaining robust legal support for mission-critical activities, satisfying both the CEO's and CFO's objectives.

Scenario IV: The Crisis

It's 7:30 p.m. on a Friday. You're about to leave for your child's school play when your phone buzzes: the CEO wants urgent legal sign-off on a new digital ad campaign for a flagship product launch. The campaign touts the product as "the only solution that works—guaranteed," and is set to go live Monday morning. The CMO is adamant that this bold language is needed to beat a major competitor, who just announced a similar launch. Meanwhile, you recall that a peer company was recently fined for misleading advertising, and social media is already abuzz with rumors about your new product.

Your Approach:
- Convene a late-night virtual meeting with marketing, compliance, and product teams to dissect the claims and identify legal vulnerabilities.
- Present real-world examples of recent regulatory crackdowns and the reputational fallout for companies caught overstating product benefits.
- Offer creative, compliant alternatives that still capture the product's value, such as customer testimonials or third-party endorsements.
- Highlight the risks of launching without proper vetting, including the potential for a viral backlash or a competitor complaint to the FTC.
- Demonstrate leadership by calmly guiding the team through a rapid risk assessment, and ensure the CEO understands both the legal and business stakes before a final decision is made.

Pro-Tip: If your CEO doesn't include you in major decisions or avoids your advice, this could indicate they don't see Legal as a strategic function. Work on building trust by aligning your advice with their priorities. This might involve attending key business meetings, offering proactive legal insights, and demonstrating a deep understanding of the company's operations.

Scenario V: Strategic GC-CFO Collaboration with CEO Engagement
Acme Corporation, a global technology firm, is preparing to launch a major new product line while navigating increased regulatory scrutiny and tightening budgets. The CEO has tasked the General Counsel (GC) and Chief Financial Officer (CFO) with ensuring the initiative advances smoothly, remains compliant, and delivers strong financial results.

Strategic Alignment and Blueprinting
The GC and CFO jointly develop a strategic blueprint that aligns the legal department's objectives with Acme's broader business goals. This includes:
- Integrating a new contract management system and legal spend management software, providing both legal and finance teams with real-time data on contract status, legal spend, and key risk indicators.
- Setting mutually agreed-upon KPIs for legal spend, contract cycle times, and compliance rates, benchmarked against peer organizations.

They present this blueprint to the CEO, emphasizing how it will streamline operations, improve risk management, and support the company's growth strategy.

Enhanced Communication and Transparency
To foster transparency, the GC and CFO establish:
- monthly joint meetings to review legal spend, discuss upcoming regulatory changes, and address emerging risks
- a shared digital workspace where both teams can access up-to-date reports, risk assessments, and scenario plans

The CEO is briefed quarterly on key legal and financial metrics, ensuring executive visibility and alignment.

Operational Efficiency and Scenario Planning
The GC implements granular expense tracking for all legal matters, categorizing costs by business unit and legal issue. Together with the CFO, they develop scenario-based budgets for the product launch:
- *Best-case.* Routine regulatory clearance, minimal disputes
- *Most likely.* Moderate regulatory engagement, some contract renegotiations
- *Worst-case.* Regulatory delays, significant litigation

These scenarios are reviewed with the CEO, who appreciates the proactive planning and clear budgetary expectations.

Risk Management and Quantification

The GC and CFO collaborate on an enterprise risk management framework that integrates legal and financial perspectives. The GC presents legal risks, such as potential IP disputes or compliance failures, in financial terms, using heat maps and quantifiable metrics to illustrate potential impacts on revenue and costs. This approach enables the CEO to make informed decisions about resource allocation and risk appetite.

Leveraging Technology and Innovation

The GC champions the adoption of an e-discovery platform and document automation tools, demonstrating measurable ROI through reduced outside counsel spend and faster contract turnaround times. A legal dashboard tracks litigation costs, compliance rates, and contract cycle times, which the CFO uses to support data-driven budgeting.

The CEO highlights these innovations in a company-wide meeting as examples of cross-functional leadership driving value.

Building a Culture of Collaboration

The GC and CFO organize regular cross-functional workshops and team-building sessions for their departments, fostering trust and understanding. They jointly lead a task force on the product launch, ensuring legal and financial considerations are integrated from the outset.

Demonstrating Value Beyond Compliance

The GC proactively identifies how improved contract negotiation and IP protection will enhance revenue and reduce risk. ROI analyses for major legal projects are presented to the CFO and CEO, showing tangible value in terms of avoided costs and increased asset value.

CEO Engagement and Impact

Throughout the process, the GC maintains a strong partnership with the CEO by:

- translating legal strategy into business outcomes, emphasizing how legal initiatives support growth, cost savings, and risk reduction
- providing clear, actionable insights that inform executive decision-making
- demonstrating leadership in cross-functional collaboration, innovation, and value creation

Outcome
The CFO recognizes the GC as a strategic advisor, not just a risk mitigator. The partnership between the GC and CFO delivers operational efficiencies, robust risk management, and measurable business value, enabling Acme Corporation to launch its new product line with confidence and competitive advantage.

By moving beyond cost control to embrace transparency, data-driven decision-making, and a culture of collaboration, GCs can become indispensable strategic partners to the CFO, helping the organization not only manage risk and control costs but also drive innovation and growth.

Final Thought: The Indispensable Advisor
Mastering the art of managing up with the CEO and CFO is essential for any General Counsel who wants to be a true strategic advisor. It requires a deep understanding of the business, strong communication skills, and the ability to balance legal risks with business opportunities. By building trust, offering solutions, and demonstrating value, you can become an indispensable advisor who shapes executive decisions and guides the company towards long-term success.

THE HOT SEAT

THREE

THE CHRO

—

STRATEGIC PARTNERING FOR PEOPLE, CULTURE,
AND COMPLIANCE

The CHRO—Strategic Partnering for People, Culture, and Compliance

A thriving organization depends on more than financial acumen or technical prowess. It requires a workplace where people feel valued, protected, and empowered. At the heart of this environment are two key leaders: the General Counsel (GC) and the Chief Human Resources Officer (CHRO). Their partnership is not just beneficial; it is essential for managing risk, cultivating talent, and shaping a culture that supports both compliance and business success.

The Chief Human Resources Officer (CHRO) is responsible for talent management, culture, and ensuring compliance with employment laws. Your collaboration with HR is crucial in managing and promoting talent in the Legal Department, mitigating risks related to workplace disputes, and ensuring corporate policies reflect the applicable legal and regulatory requirements. A strong partnership can foster a positive and compliant workplace.

How to Work with the CHRO

Ensure Compliance with Labor Laws
Employment law violations can lead to costly litigation and reputational damage. Stay up-to-date on the latest labor laws and regulations and advise HR on how to ensure compliance.

Collaborate on Workplace Investigations
Whether it's harassment claims, discrimination issues, or whistleblower complaints, you must work together with HR. Develop clear protocols for conducting investigations and ensure that they are handled fairly and impartially.

Support Change Management
Mergers, layoffs, and executive transitions require strong HR and legal alignment to avoid missteps. Work with HR to develop communication plans, severance agreements, and other documents to ensure a smooth transition.

Manage and Promote Talent in the Legal Department
Partner with HR to develop and implement talent management and promotion opportunities within legal, in order to retain the talent you need to make legal shine.

Develop Clear and Consistent HR Policies
Work with HR to develop HR policies that are clear, concise, and consistent with applicable laws and regulations.

Let's explore how the GC can work together with the CHRO to advance these goals.

Ensuring Compliance with Labor Laws: The General Counsel's Role

Employment law compliance is a critical responsibility for any organization, as violations can lead to costly litigation and reputational harm. The GC plays a central role in ensuring the company adheres to labor laws and regulations, working closely with HR to build robust compliance programs that protect both the company and its employees.

Key Responsibilities of the GC in Labor Law Compliance
- Regularly review HR policies and procedures for legal compliance. The GC must stay informed about the latest changes in employment law, including new regulations and court decisions, and ensure all company policies reflect these updates.
- Provide timely, practical legal advice to HR and management. This includes advising on hiring practices, wage and hour laws, leave entitlements, workplace safety, and disciplinary actions.
- Train HR staff and managers in new legal developments. Ongoing education is essential to ensure all relevant personnel understand their obligations and can spot potential issues before they escalate.
- Require legal review of major HR decisions and disciplinary actions. Legal oversight helps prevent inadvertent violations and strengthens the defensibility of employment decisions if challenged.
- Conduct or oversee internal investigations into employment-related complaints, such as harassment or discrimination, to ensure fair processes and compliance with legal standards.

Collaboration Between Legal and HR

Effective compliance depends on strong collaboration between the GC and the Chief Human Resources Officer (CHRO). This partnership can include:
- Jointly developing and updating compliance programs, including standardized review processes and personnel improvement plans

- Coordinating responses to employee complaints and legal holds, ensuring documentation is thorough and accessible for potential litigation or regulatory inquiries
- Aligning on risk mitigation strategies that both reduce legal exposure and promote a positive workplace culture

Proactive Compliance Strategies
- Conduct regular audits of HR practices, such as wage and hour audits, to identify and address compliance gaps before they result in violations or lawsuits.
- Utilize external resources, such as employment law seminars and compliance checklists, to benchmark and improve internal policies and practices.
- Integrate employment law requirements into the company's code of conduct and broader compliance framework, ensuring a unified approach to legal and ethical standards.

Collaborating on Workplace Investigations

Harassment claims, discrimination allegations, and whistleblower complaints demand a coordinated response. The GC and CHRO must develop clear protocols for conducting investigations that are fair, impartial, and well-documented. This partnership ensures:
- investigations are handled consistently and transparently
- legal and regulatory obligations are met
- the company's culture of trust and accountability is reinforced

When a workplace complaint arises, the effectiveness of the investigation process depends on a seamless partnership between the GC and CHRO. Each brings distinct expertise: the GC ensures legal compliance and risk mitigation, while the CHRO brings deep knowledge of organizational culture, employee relations, and HR best practices. This collaboration is essential for several reasons:

Establishing Clear Protocols and Roles

A jointly developed investigation protocol should outline:

- immediate steps to protect involved parties and prevent retaliation
- criteria for selecting an impartial investigator, often favoring HR professionals for their policy expertise and perceived neutrality
- the scope, timeline, and documentation standards for the investigation

By working together, the GC and CHRO ensure that investigations are not only thorough but also defensible if later scrutinized by regulators or in litigation.

Ensuring Fairness and Consistency

A structured, repeatable process, co-designed by legal and HR, demonstrates the organization's commitment to fairness. This consistency:

- reduces the risk of bias or the perception of favoritism
- provides a reliable framework for handling sensitive interviews, evidence collection, and reporting
- builds trust among employees, who see that complaints are taken seriously and handled impartially

Balancing Legal and Human Considerations

The GC and CHRO must balance legal requirements (such as confidentiality, privilege, and regulatory reporting) with the human dimensions of employee relations. For example:

- The GC advises on legal risks, regulatory obligations, and privilege considerations, ensuring the company's response meets all statutory requirements.
- The CHRO manages communication with employees, supports those involved, and addresses broader cultural or systemic issues revealed by the investigation.

Leveraging Technology and Data

Modern case management systems, often implemented by HR with legal oversight, help standardize documentation, track outcomes, and ensure transparency. These tools:

- streamline intake, evidence tracking, and reporting
- provide analytics to identify patterns and systemic risks
- support defensible, data-driven decision-making

Reinforcing Organizational Values
Effective GC-CHRO collaboration models the company's values of integrity, respect, and accountability. By handling investigations with professionalism and transparency, they:
- foster a culture where employees feel safe to report concerns
- demonstrate leadership's commitment to ethical conduct
  and compliance
- reduce reputational and legal risks for the organization

Joint reviews of completed investigations allow the GC and CHRO to identify process improvements, address recurring issues, and adapt protocols to evolving legal and cultural expectations. Regular training for investigators, clear communication with stakeholders, and a willingness to learn from each case further strengthen the partnership and the organization's overall resilience.

Supporting Change Management

Major organizational changes—such as mergers, layoffs, and executive transitions—demand seamless coordination between the General Counsel (GC) and Chief Human Resources Officer (CHRO). Their partnership is essential for both legal compliance and maintaining a positive employee experience during periods of uncertainty. Below is an expanded look at how GCs and CHROs can work together to support effective change management:

Developing Clear and Compliant Communication Plans
- The GC and CHRO should jointly craft communication strategies
  that are not only transparent and empathetic but also compliant with
  all relevant employment laws and regulations. This includes ensuring

messaging aligns with federal statutes such as the WARN Act, ADA, and Title VII, and is sensitive to the needs of diverse employee populations[2].

- By coordinating communications, they can prevent misinformation, reduce anxiety, and build trust. The CHRO brings insight into employee sentiment and cultural nuances, while the GC ensures statements do not expose the organization to legal risk.
- During CEO or C-suite transitions, the CHRO often acts as a bridge between the board, executive team, and employees, coordinating the onboarding process and initial communications to foster stability and confidence.

Drafting Severance Agreements and Transition Documents

- The GC and CHRO collaborate to develop severance agreements, retention packages, and other transition documents that are fair, legally sound, and tailored to the organization's strategic goals.
- This partnership ensures that all documents comply with applicable laws (such as ERISA, COBRA, and local labor regulations) and reflect the organization's values, reducing the risk of disputes or litigation.
- In the context of mergers or restructuring, the CHRO's understanding of workforce dynamics and the GC's legal oversight are both critical for negotiating terms that protect the organization while treating employees with respect.

Anticipating and Mitigating Legal Risks

- Proactive risk assessment is a joint responsibility. The GC identifies potential legal pitfalls, such as discrimination claims, contract breaches, or union grievances, while the CHRO evaluates the impact on employee morale and culture.
- Together, they conduct due diligence on workforce capabilities, review employment contracts, and harmonize HR policies to ensure compliance and smooth integration, especially during M&A activities.

---

2 https://www.shrm.org/topics-tools/tools/toolkits/managing-organizational-change

- They also monitor emerging risks related to diversity, equity, and inclusion (DE&I), and environmental, social, and governance (ESG) standards, areas that are increasingly scrutinized by boards and regulators.

Facilitating Leadership Assessment and Succession Planning
- During executive transitions, the CHRO leads leadership assessments and succession planning, with the GC ensuring the process adheres to governance standards and confidentiality requirements.
- This collaboration helps identify and prepare future leaders, maintaining organizational continuity and confidence during change.

Ensuring Business Continuity and Employee Well-Being
- The CHRO and GC work together to harmonize HR operations, such as payroll and benefits, and to create contingency plans that ensure uninterrupted services during organizational transitions.
- They use feedback mechanisms, such as surveys and focus groups, to monitor morale and adjust strategies as needed, reinforcing a culture of transparency and support.

Building a Foundation of Trust
- Open communication, transparency, and mutual respect are the cornerstones of a successful GC-CHRO partnership. When these leaders present a united front, they not only mitigate legal and operational risks but also foster employee engagement and retention, even in turbulent times.

Managing and Promoting Legal Talent

The collaboration between the General Counsel (GC) and the Chief Human Resources Officer (CHRO) is increasingly recognized as a strategic driver for building a high-performing, future-ready legal department. By leveraging HR's expertise in talent management, the GC can elevate the legal function beyond traditional boundaries and ensure it is fully aligned with the business's evolving needs.

Developing and Implementing Promotion Pathways and Retention Strategies
- The CHRO brings deep experience in designing career frameworks, performance management systems, and retention programs. By working together, the GC and CHRO can establish transparent promotion pathways for legal staff, ensuring clear criteria for advancement and professional growth.
- Jointly, they can implement tailored development plans, mentorship programs, and succession planning for key legal roles, drawing on HR's best practices and the GC's understanding of the unique competencies required for legal excellence
- Regular talent reviews, often led by HR, can be expanded to include legal staff, ensuring that high-potential legal professionals are recognized and nurtured for future leadership roles.

Building a High-Performing Legal Team that Supports the Business
- By collaborating with HR, the GC can shift the legal department's role from a reactive advisor to a proactive business partner. This includes embedding legal professionals within business units and encouraging them to develop broader business acumen and soft skills.
- The GC and CHRO can jointly define the competencies needed for legal team members to succeed as strategic partners, such as risk assessment, adaptability, and commercial awareness.
- Cross-functional training and regular joint policy reviews between HR and legal staff foster mutual understanding and enable the legal team to better anticipate and address business needs.
- The partnership also enables the legal department to contribute to organizational initiatives beyond legal compliance, such as employee well-being, workplace safety, and culture-building—thereby increasing its visibility and impact across the company.

Additional Benefits of GC–CHRO Collaboration
Succession Planning. The GC and CHRO often collaborate on succession planning for senior legal roles and even for the C-suite, ensuring continuity and preparedness for leadership transitions.

Employee Experience. Their partnership is central to shaping a positive employee experience within the legal department, which is crucial for attracting and retaining top legal talent in a competitive market.

Reputation and Influence. As the legal department becomes more integrated with HR and the broader business, its reputation shifts from being a gatekeeper to being an enabler and trusted advisor, opening new pathways for career growth and influence within the organization.

Developing Clear and Consistent HR Policies

Ambiguous or outdated HR policies can create confusion, erode employee trust, and expose the organization to significant legal and reputational risks. To mitigate these issues, the General Counsel (GC) and Chief Human Resources Officer (CHRO) must establish a robust partnership focused on developing, maintaining, and communicating effective HR policies.

Collaborative Policy Drafting
- The GC and HR should jointly draft policies to ensure they are concise, clear, and fully aligned with the latest federal, state, and local laws. This collaboration leverages the GC's legal expertise and HR's understanding of organizational culture and operational needs.
- Policies should address not only legal compliance but also reflect the organization's values, diversity and inclusion goals, and ethical standards.

Ongoing Policy Review and Updates
- Laws and regulations affecting employment are constantly evolving. The GC should regularly monitor legal developments and proactively inform HR of relevant changes.
- Together, the GC and HR should establish a formal schedule for reviewing all HR policies, such as annually or semi-annually, and implement a process for ad hoc updates when urgent legal changes arise.

- This review process should include benchmarking against
  industry standards and best practices to ensure competitiveness
  and compliance.

Effective Communication and Training

Clear communication of policy changes is essential to ensure understanding and compliance across the organization. The GC and HR should collaborate on a communication plan that includes:
- timely announcements of policy updates through multiple channels
  (e.g., email, intranet, team meetings)
- explanations of the rationale behind changes to foster buy-in and
  reduce resistance
- accessible documentation, such as FAQs or summary guides, to help
  employees easily understand new or revised policies
- regular training sessions should be conducted to educate managers
  and employees on policy requirements, with special attention to areas
  of high legal risk (e.g., anti-harassment, workplace safety, data privacy)

Feedback and Continuous Improvement

- The GC and HR should encourage feedback from employees and
  managers regarding policy clarity and effectiveness.
- Establishing mechanisms for collecting and addressing questions or
  concerns helps identify ambiguities or gaps that may require further
  clarification or revision.
- This feedback loop supports a culture of transparency and continuous
  improvement, reducing the likelihood of misunderstandings or
  non-compliance.

By working together in these areas, the GC and CHRO can ensure that HR policies are not only legally sound but also practical, well-understood, and consistently applied throughout the organization. This partnership strengthens organizational resilience and fosters a fair, compliant, and high-performing workplace.

Five-Point Framework for Effective General Counsel Collaboration with the Chief Human Resources Officer

1. Joint Compliance and Risk Management
- Regularly review and update HR policies and procedures to ensure alignment with evolving labor and employment laws.
- Co-develop robust compliance programs, conduct regular audits, and integrate legal requirements into the company's code of conduct.
- Provide ongoing legal education to HR and management, ensuring that all stakeholders understand their obligations and can identify potential risks before they escalate.
- Require legal review of major HR decisions and disciplinary actions to prevent inadvertent violations and strengthen defensibility if challenged.

2. Collaborative Workplace Investigations
- Establish clear, jointly developed protocols for handling workplace complaints (e.g., harassment, discrimination, whistleblower reports).
- Assign impartial investigators, balancing legal standards for fairness with HR's understanding of employee relations and organizational culture.
- Ensure thorough documentation, confidentiality, and compliance with legal and regulatory obligations throughout the investigation process.
- Jointly review findings, determine appropriate actions, and communicate outcomes while maintaining trust and transparency with employees.

3. Strategic Change Management and Communication
- Co-create communication plans for major organizational changes (e.g., mergers, layoffs, executive transitions) that are transparent, empathetic, and legally compliant.

- Draft severance agreements, retention packages, and transition documents together, ensuring both legal soundness and alignment with organizational values.
- Anticipate and mitigate legal and cultural risks by conducting joint risk assessments and harmonizing HR policies, especially during periods of significant change.

4. Talent Management and Legal Team Development

- Collaborate on promotion pathways, succession planning, and retention strategies for legal talent, leveraging HR's expertise in career frameworks and performance management.
- Conduct joint talent reviews, design development programs, and implement mentorship initiatives to build a high-performing, business-savvy legal team.
- Use HR's tools (e.g., engagement surveys, stay interviews) to monitor morale and address issues impacting legal staff, ensuring the legal function is fully integrated into broader talent strategies.

5. Continuous Policy Improvement and Cultural Alignment

- Jointly draft, review, and update HR policies to ensure clarity, legal compliance, and alignment with organizational values, diversity, and inclusion goals.
- Communicate policy changes effectively, using multiple channels and providing accessible documentation and training for managers and employees.
- Establish feedback mechanisms to capture employee input, identify ambiguities, and drive continuous improvement in policies and practices.
- Model open communication, trust, and collaborative leadership, reinforcing a culture of integrity, accountability, and cross-functional partnership throughout the organization.

This framework ensures the GC–CHRO partnership is proactive, aligned, and strategic, driving both compliance and a positive, resilient workplace culture.

Case Studies

Scenario I: Your Partner in People & Culture

HR is fast-tracking a new performance management system featuring subjective peer reviews and "stack ranking." The CHRO wants to roll it out before the next earnings call to showcase a "culture of accountability." Employees, already anxious after recent layoffs, fear the new system will be biased. Meanwhile, the company is still under a consent decree from a past discrimination lawsuit, and a labor union is threatening to go public with concerns.

Your Approach:

- Collaborate with HR to build objective criteria and robust documentation protocols into the new system.
- Recommend bias-awareness and anti-retaliation training for all managers and reviewers.
- Propose regular legal audits of performance data to spot patterns of potential discrimination.
- Develop a confidential appeals process for employees and communicate it clearly to build trust.
- Step in as a leader to mediate between HR's desire for speed and employees' need for fairness, ensuring the system supports rather than undermines company culture and compliance.

Pro-Tip: If HR operates without legal oversight on major decisions, you risk non-compliance and employee lawsuits. Ensure all HR policies and disciplinary actions comply with legal best practices. This might involve reviewing all HR policies and procedures, providing training to HR staff on legal compliance, and requiring legal review of all major HR decisions.

Key Takeaways

- Work proactively with HR to develop robust compliance programs.
- Ensure employee policies align with legal and ethical best practices.
- Assist HR in crafting effective response strategies for workplace disputes.
- Promote DEI initiatives and foster a culture of inclusion in the workplace.
- Develop clear and consistent HR policies that comply with applicable laws and regulations.

Scenario II: Sexual Harassment Complaint Against a Supervisor

Eleanor, an administrative assistant, reports to Human Resources that her direct supervisor, Devin, has repeatedly made inappropriate comments about her appearance and has asked her out on dates multiple times, despite her clear refusals. Eleanor feels uncomfortable and fears retaliation if she continues to reject Devin's advances or pursues a formal complaint. She is also concerned about the impact on her job security and career advancement.

Collaborative Approach: GC and CHRO Partnership

1. Initial Assessment and Immediate Actions

CHRO. Receives the complaint from Eleanor and ensures she is safe from immediate retaliation or further harassment. The CHRO provides Eleanor with information about her rights, support resources, and the company's non-retaliation policy.

GC. Advises on legal obligations, including prompt action under Title VII and any relevant state laws, and ensures that all steps taken are documented to preserve legal privilege where appropriate.

2. Assigning an Impartial Investigator

CHRO. Selects an investigator who is not in Eleanor's reporting line and has no prior involvement with Devin to ensure impartiality. This may be a senior HR professional or an external investigator if necessary.

GC. Reviews the selection to avoid any conflicts of interest and ensures that the investigator is trained in both company policy and legal requirements regarding harassment investigations.

3. Developing an Investigation Plan

CHRO & GC. Collaborate to outline the scope of the investigation, including:
- Who will be interviewed (complainant, accused, witnesses)
- What evidence will be collected (emails, messages, performance reviews)
- Timelines for each stage of the process
- The GC ensures the plan complies with legal standards for fairness and thoroughness, while the CHRO ensures the plan aligns with company policies and values.

4. Conducting the Investigation

Investigator (overseen by CHRO and GC). Conducts confidential interviews, collects documentation, and maintains detailed records of findings.

GC. Provides legal guidance on privilege, confidentiality, and how to handle sensitive information, particularly if there is a risk of litigation or regulatory inquiry.

CHRO. Ensures that all parties are treated respectfully and that the investigation process is communicated clearly to both the complainant and the accused.

5. Reaching a Conclusion and Taking Action

GC & CHRO. Review the investigator's findings together. The GC evaluates legal risks and compliance, while the CHRO considers organizational impact and employee relations.

Action. If the complaint is substantiated, the GC and CHRO jointly determine appropriate disciplinary action, corrective measures, and steps to prevent recurrence (such as additional training or policy updates).

6. Communication and Documentation

CHRO. Communicates the outcome to Eleanor and Devin, providing a written summary of the investigation's findings and actions taken, while maintaining confidentiality as required by law.

GC. Ensures that all documentation is complete and stored securely in case of future legal proceedings.

7. Monitoring and Follow-up

CHRO. Checks in with Eleanor periodically to ensure there is no retaliation and that she feels safe and supported.

GC. Monitors for any legal developments, such as external complaints or lawsuits, and advises on ongoing compliance.

This collaborative approach ensures that workplace investigations are handled with both legal rigor and a human-centered perspective, protecting the organization and its employees while reinforcing a culture of trust and accountability.

Key Takeaway
When the GC and CHRO collaborate closely on workplace investigations, they create a process that is not only compliant and defensible but also trusted by employees and aligned with the company's broader mission and values.

Scenario III: CEO Succession and Organizational Culture Shift
A large, public company faces the sudden retirement of its long-time CEO. The board wants to use this transition as an opportunity to refresh its leadership culture. However, there are concerns about legal risks around executive contracts, potential internal unrest, and the need for clear, unified communication to employees and external stakeholders.

How the GC and CHRO Can Collaborate

1. *Joint Succession Planning and Board Engagement*
   - The CHRO leads the executive committee talent review, working closely with the CEO and board on succession planning, including identifying internal and external candidates aligned with the company's cultural goals.
   - The GC is involved in governance-related scenarios (e.g., if the CEO becomes incapacitated) and reviews all legal aspects of the succession process, including employment contracts, non-compete clauses, and regulatory disclosures.
   - Both collaborate on preparing proxy statements and board communications, ensuring transparency and compliance.

2. *Unified Communication Strategy*
   - The GC and CHRO co-develop communication plans for employees, investors, and the public, balancing transparency with legal and reputational risk management.
   - They ensure messaging is compliant with disclosure requirements and sensitive to employee concerns, reinforcing trust and stability during the transition.
   - By presenting a united front, they model collaborative leadership and set the tone for the new culture.

3. *Culture Integration*
   - The CHRO drives the assessment of leadership candidates with an eye toward advancing inclusive leadership, leveraging insights from employee engagement surveys and talent analytics.
   - The GC ensures that all hiring and promotion processes are legally defensible and free from bias, providing legal guidance on any changes to policies or practices.
   - Together, they shape and communicate new or revised cultural initiatives, ensuring they are both impactful and compliant.

4. Risk Assessment and Mitigation
- The GC identifies legal risks related to executive transition, such as contract disputes, severance obligations, and potential litigation from internal candidates who are passed over.
- The CHRO evaluates the impact of leadership changes on morale, retention, and culture, developing support programs for employees and managers.
- They jointly create contingency plans for possible scenarios, such as negative media coverage or employee activism, ensuring the organization is prepared to respond effectively.

5. Ongoing Monitoring and Feedback
- After the transition, the CHRO and GC regularly review the effectiveness of new policies, monitor employee sentiment, and address any emerging issues.
- They provide updates to the board and executive team, ensuring continuous alignment and improvement.

Key Collaboration Traits Demonstrated

Open communication and trust. The GC and CHRO maintain regular, candid dialogue, sharing insights and concerns to anticipate challenges and opportunities.

Non-territorial mindset. Both leaders focus on what is best for the company, leveraging each other's expertise and modeling collaborative behavior for their teams.

Holistic perspective. By combining legal risk assessment with a deep understanding of people and culture, they provide the board and executive team with well-rounded recommendations that support both compliance and employee engagement.

Key Takeaway

By integrating their expertise, the GC and CHRO help the organization navigate complex changes smoothly, avoid costly missteps, and maintain a resilient, motivated workforce. Their collaboration is not only about compliance; it is a strategic driver of successful transformation.

Scenario IV: Advancing High-Potential Legal Talent Through GC–CHRO Collaboration

A multinational manufacturing company is experiencing rapid growth and faces increasing regulatory complexity. The General Counsel (GC) has identified several high-potential attorneys within the legal department, but is concerned about limited promotion pathways and the risk of losing top talent to external opportunities. The Chief Human Resources Officer (CHRO) is simultaneously leading a company-wide initiative to strengthen internal talent pipelines and align leadership development with the company's inclusion goals.

The CEO tasks the GC and CHRO to collaborate on identifying, developing, and advancing legal talent to ensure the legal department is equipped to support the company's evolving needs.

How the GC and CHRO Collaborate

1. Joint Talent Assessment and Succession Planning
  - The GC and CHRO initiate a comprehensive talent review of the legal department, using HR's structured assessment tools to evaluate not only technical legal skills but also leadership potential, business acumen, and alignment with company values.
  - Together, they identify high-potential attorneys and map out succession plans for key legal roles, ensuring continuity and readiness for future leadership needs.

2. Designing Promotion Pathways and Development Programs
  - Drawing on HR's experience in career pathing, the CHRO helps the GC create transparent promotion criteria tailored to legal roles, clarifying what competencies and achievements are required for advancement.
  - The CHRO introduces leadership development programs, such as cross-functional projects, executive mentorship, and stretch assignments, to help legal professionals build broader business and management skills.
  - The GC provides ongoing coaching and feedback, leveraging HR's performance management frameworks to ensure regular, constructive conversations about career growth.

3. Enhancing Retention and Engagement
- The CHRO works with the GC to conduct "stay interviews" and engagement surveys with legal staff, identifying factors that drive satisfaction and areas for improvement.
- Together, they address any issues related to workload, recognition, or career development, leveraging HR's expertise in employee experience and well-being.
- The GC and CHRO jointly communicate the new talent development initiatives, reinforcing the company's commitment to investing in legal professionals' growth.

4. Reporting to Leadership and the Board
- The GC and CHRO prepare joint updates for the executive team and board, highlighting progress on legal talent development, succession planning, and DEI goals.[3]
- Their unified approach demonstrates to leadership that the legal department is not only a risk manager but also a source of future business leaders.

Primary Outcomes
- clearer career pathways within the legal department, reducing turnover and increasing engagement among high-potential attorneys
- stronger succession plans or critical legal roles, ensuring business continuity and readiness for future challenges
- a high-performing, business-savvy legal team that is better equipped to partner with the business and drive strategic growth

Key Takeaway
The GC–CHRO partnership is essential for managing and promoting legal talent in a way that aligns with organizational strategy, fosters diversity and inclusion, and builds a legal team that is both high-performing and deeply connected to the business's success.

---

3 https://www.mlaglobal.com/en/insights/articles/success-factors-for-effective-general-counsel?byconsultantorauthor=amy-katz

Scenario V: Navigating Performance Management Reform

Suppose HR is fast-tracking a new performance management system featuring subjective peer reviews and "stack ranking." The CHRO wants to launch before the next earnings call to showcase a "culture of accountability." Employees, still anxious after layoffs, fear bias in the new system. The company remains under a consent decree from a past discrimination lawsuit, and a labor union is raising public concerns.

The collaboration between the General Counsel (GC) and Chief Human Resources Officer (CHRO) in this scenario requires balancing legal compliance, employee trust, and strategic business objectives. Here's how they can address the challenges:

1. Legal Risk Assessment and Compliance Alignment

GC Role
- Review the proposed performance system against the **consent decree** obligations and anti-discrimination laws (e.g., Title VII, ADA). Subjective peer reviews and stack ranking risk amplifying bias, which could violate the decree or trigger new litigation.
- Advise on **documentation standards** to ensure transparency in evaluations, reducing exposure to discrimination claims.

CHRO Role
- Delay the rollout until the GC validates the system's compliance. Fast-tracking without legal review risks exacerbating union concerns and regulatory penalties.
- Partner with the GC to design **bias-mitigation safeguards,** such as calibrated training for reviewers and AI tools to flag inconsistent ratings.

Joint Action
- Conduct a mock audit of the system using historical data to identify potential disparities in ratings across protected groups.

2. Mitigating Bias and Building Trust

GC/CHRO Collaboration
- Replace purely subjective peer reviews with **structured, competency-based criteria** tied to measurable job outcomes. For example, define "accountability" using specific behavioral indicators (e.g., meeting deadlines, collaborative problem-solving).

- Implement **360-degree feedback** with anonymity protections to reduce retaliation fears and aggregate input from diverse sources.

Employee Communication
- Co-develop FAQs and training sessions to explain how the system aligns with legal requirements and fairness standards. Highlight the GC's role in oversight to reassure employees.
- Publicly commit to **transparent reporting** on rating distribution and demographic impacts, addressing union concerns about systemic bias.

3. Strategic Timing and Stakeholder Management

GC Role
- Advise the CHRO and CEO on the risks of prioritizing earnings deadlines over compliance. A rushed launch could undermine the consent decree's progress and attract regulatory scrutiny.

CHRO Role
- Propose a **phased rollout** (e.g., pilot teams) to demonstrate progress to investors while allowing time for adjustments. Frame this as "building a sustainable culture of accountability" in earnings communications.

Union Engagement
- Jointly meet with union representatives to outline safeguards (e.g., third-party audits of ratings, grievance mechanisms). Position the GC as a neutral arbiter to defuse tensions.

4. Long-Term Cultural Integration
- Establish a **GC-CHRO task force** to monitor the system's impact on retention, morale, and legal risk. For example, track whether stack ranking increases attrition in protected groups.

Key Takeaway
By merging legal rigor with HR's operational focus, the GC and CHRO can transform a high-risk initiative into a model for compliant, equitable performance management.

Final Thought—Culture is Risk

If you wait until an issue is "legal," you're already late.

Culture, talent decisions, investigations, and change management are where risk is created—or contained—long before a lawsuit, regulator, or headline appears. That makes the CHRO one of your most important strategic partners, whether the organization realizes it or not.

The best General Counsels don't treat HR as a downstream function or a cleanup crew. They embed legal judgment upstream—into hiring, performance systems, investigations, and transitions—where it *actually* matters. They help HR get decisions right the first time, not just defensible after the fact.

Get this partnership right, and you reduce risk, build trust, and strengthen the company's spine. Get it wrong, and you'll spend years managing consequences that never had to exist.

People are strategy. Culture is risk. Ignore either at your peril.

FOUR

THE BOARD OF DIRECTORS

—

BUILDING CREDIBILITY AND EARNING TRUST

The Board of Directors— Building Credibility and Earning Trust

You've made it to the big leagues—working with the board of directors. This is where strategy meets oversight, where high-stakes decisions unfold, and where your ability to command respect and credibility will define your success.

Building credibility with the board isn't about dazzling them with legal jargon or reciting regulations; it's about being the person they trust when things go sideways. Your job isn't just to provide legal advice; it's to translate complex issues into clear, actionable insights that help directors fulfill their fiduciary duties without losing sleep at night.

So, how do you earn that trust? Let's break it down.

Ten Key Strategies for Surviving and Thriving

1. Speak Their Language (Hint: It's Not Legalese)

Boards don't want law school lectures. They want clarity, risk assessments, and a path forward. They're not interested in a case citation; they want to know what it means for the company and how they should respond. Communicating effectively with the board requires understanding their priorities, speaking their language, and delivering information in a concise and actionable manner.

a. Lead with Business Impact

When presenting an issue, frame it in terms of business consequences: "If we take this approach, we mitigate the risk of X and align with industry standards, but we may face pushback from Y." This approach helps directors understand the direct implications of legal matters on the company's overall performance and strategic goals. By quantifying the potential risks and rewards, you enable them to make informed decisions that align with the company's objectives.

Quantify the Impact. Whenever possible, translate legal risks into financial terms. For example, instead of saying "There is a risk of litigation," say "This action could lead to litigation with potential damages of $X million."

Connect to Strategic Goals. Explain how the legal issue impacts the company's strategic objectives. For instance, "This new regulation could delay our product launch by six months, impacting our revenue projections for the year."

Use Visual Aids. Use charts, graphs, and other visual aids to illustrate the business impact of legal matters. This can help directors quickly grasp complex information and make informed decisions.

b. Get to the Point

Directors juggle dozens of priorities. If you can't summarize your key message in two minutes, refine your approach. Time is a precious commodity for board members, who are often juggling multiple responsibilities and commitments. To effectively communicate with them, it is essential to be concise, focused, and respectful of their time.

The Elevator Pitch. Develop a concise summary of each legal issue that you can deliver in under two minutes. This should include the key facts, potential risks, and your recommended course of action.

Executive Summaries. Provide executive summaries at the beginning of all written materials. These summaries should highlight the key points and provide a clear overview of the issue.

Prioritize Information. Focus on the most important information and avoid getting bogged down in unnecessary details.

Practice Your Delivery. Rehearse your presentations to ensure that you can deliver your message in a clear and concise manner.

c. Numbers Matter

When possible, quantify the legal risk—potential fines, probability of litigation, or historical precedent in financial terms. Numbers provide concrete data that directors can use to assess the potential impact of legal matters on the company's financial performance and shareholder value.

Potential Fine. Estimate the potential fines and penalties associated with non-compliance.

Probability of Litigation. Assess the likelihood of litigation based on historical data and industry trends.

Historical Precedent. Provide examples of similar cases and their financial outcomes.

Return on Investment. Calculate the potential return on investment for legal initiatives, such as compliance programs or risk management strategies.

d. Build and Leverage Relationships

Strong relationships are the foundation of effective boardroom influence. By proactively connecting with directors and key stakeholders, you establish trust, credibility, and open lines of communication. These relationships not only help you anticipate concerns and align legal advice with business priorities but also position you as a valued partner in strategic decision-making.

Identify Key Stakeholders. Map out the individuals and departments most affected by legal issues, such as finance, operations, compliance, and business unit leaders. Engage them early to understand their priorities and concerns.

Foster Trust and Credibility. Build rapport by consistently providing practical, business-oriented legal advice. Demonstrate a clear understanding of the company's operations and strategic goals to position yourself as a trusted advisor rather than just a legal gatekeeper.

Communicate Proactively. Maintain regular, open lines of communication with directors and key executives. Share legal updates, emerging risks, and industry trends before they become urgent issues.

Collaborate Cross-Functionally. Work closely with other departments to develop holistic solutions that balance legal risk with business objectives. Participate in cross-functional meetings and projects to integrate legal insights into broader company initiatives.

Leverage Informal Networks. Cultivate informal relationships with decision-makers and influencers throughout the organization. These connections can provide valuable insights and help advance legal recommendations more effectively.

Support Board Education. Offer briefings or training sessions on emerging legal topics relevant to the board's oversight responsibilities. This positions the legal function as a proactive partner in risk management and strategic planning.

Seek Feedback and Adapt. Regularly solicit feedback from directors and executives on your communication style and legal advice. Use this input to refine your approach and better align with the board's expectations and the company's evolving needs.

e. Command the Room

Boardrooms are high-stakes environments where confidence, clarity, and presence matter as much as content. To ensure your message resonates and your recommendations are taken seriously, it's essential to project authority and engage your audience effectively.

Project Confidence. Speak clearly and assertively, making eye contact with directors. Maintain an upright posture and use purposeful gestures to reinforce your points.

Own Your Expertise. Demonstrate deep knowledge of the subject matter. Be prepared to answer tough questions and back up your recommendations with data and precedent.

Read the Room. Pay attention to nonverbal cues from directors. Adjust your tone, pace, or level of detail based on their reactions to keep them engaged.

Handle Pushback Gracefully. Respond to challenging questions or skepticism with composure. Acknowledge concerns, provide thoughtful answers, and avoid becoming defensive.

Use Storytelling. Illustrate complex legal issues with real-world examples or analogies. A compelling narrative can make your message more memorable and persuasive.

Control the Flow. Guide discussions by setting clear agendas, summarizing key points, and steering conversations back to the main objectives if they stray off course.

Close with Impact. End your presentations with a strong, actionable summary. Clearly state your recommendation and the next steps, leaving directors with a sense of direction and confidence in your guidance.

f. Enable the Board to Decide

Directors are ultimately responsible for making informed, strategic decisions. Your role is to equip them with the clarity, context, and actionable options they need to fulfill this responsibility efficiently and confidently.

Present Clear Options. Lay out distinct courses of action, highlighting the pros, cons, and potential outcomes of each. Avoid overwhelming the board with excessive detail or too many alternatives.

Clarify Decision Points. Clearly state what decision is required of the board and why it matters. Frame the issue so directors understand the urgency and significance.

Summarize Key Facts. Distill complex information into concise, digestible summaries. Use executive summaries, bullet points, or visual aids to reinforce the most important considerations.

Highlight Risks and Mitigations. Transparently outline the risks associated with each option and propose practical mitigation strategies. This empowers directors to weigh risk against reward.

Facilitate Discussion. Encourage questions and dialogue, ensuring all perspectives are considered. Guide the conversation to keep it focused on the decision at hand.

Provide a Recommendation. Offer a clear, well-supported recommendation based on your legal and business analysis. Explain your rationale to help directors understand your perspective.

Support Follow-Through. Outline next steps and any actions required post-decision. Ensure directors know what to expect and how progress will be tracked or reported.

2. Be the Voice of Reason (Not Doom)

Directors appreciate a general counsel who understands the difference between a real risk and a theoretical one. If every issue is "mission-critical" and "urgent," they'll stop taking you seriously. Maintaining credibility with the board requires providing balanced and objective assessments of legal risks, avoiding alarmist language, and offering practical solutions.

a. Pick Your Battles

Focus on the risks that truly matter. If it's a regulatory headache but not an existential crisis, put it in context. Prioritize the legal issues that have the greatest potential impact on the company's financial performance, reputation, and strategic goals.

Risk Assessment Matrix. Use a risk assessment matrix to evaluate the likelihood and impact of different legal risks.

Focus on High-Priority Risks. Concentrate your efforts on mitigating the risks that fall into the high-likelihood and high-impact categories.

Contextualize Risks. Provide context for each risk, explaining its potential impact on the company and its likelihood of occurring.

Communicate Proactively. Keep the board informed of emerging risks, even if they are not yet critical.

b. Offer Solutions, Not Just Problems

Never bring a legal issue to the board without a proposed course of action. Directors expect the general counsel to not only identify legal risks but also to provide practical solutions that mitigate those risks while aligning with the company's business objectives.

Develop Actionable Recommendations. Provide specific, actionable recommendations that the board can implement to address the legal issue.

Evaluate Alternatives. Present a range of alternative solutions, along with their potential benefits and drawbacks.

Align with Business Objectives. Ensure that your recommendations align with the company's overall business objectives and strategic goals.

Consider Feasibility. Consider the feasibility of implementing your recommendations, considering factors such as cost, resources, and timing.

c. Balance Caution with Pragmatism

The best lawyers help boards navigate risk, not paralyze them with fear. Effective legal counsel involves finding a balance between caution and pragmatism, providing guidance that allows the board to make informed decisions without being paralyzed by fear of potential legal consequences.

Assess Risk Tolerance. Understand the company's risk tolerance and tailor your advice accordingly.

Provide Realistic Assessments. Provide realistic assessments of the potential risks and rewards associated with each course of action.

Focus on Mitigation. Focus on mitigating the risks rather than eliminating them altogether.

Encourage Innovation. Encourage innovation and calculated risk-taking, while ensuring that the company remains within legal and ethical boundaries.

3. Build Relationships Beyond the Boardroom

Trust isn't built in meetings alone—it's built in the moments before and after. Building strong relationships with board members outside of formal meetings is essential for establishing trust, understanding their individual concerns, and tailoring your advice to their needs.

a. Engage with Directors One-on-One

Understanding their individual concerns and priorities helps tailor your advice. Taking the time to meet with directors individually allows you to gain a deeper understanding of their perspectives, priorities, and concerns, enabling you to provide more tailored and effective legal advice.

Regular Meetings. Schedule regular one-on-one meetings with each director to discuss their concerns and priorities.

Listen Actively. Listen actively to their concerns and ask clarifying questions to ensure that you fully understand their perspectives.

Tailor Your Advice. Tailor your legal advice to address their specific concerns and priorities.

Follow Up. Follow up after each meeting to ensure that their concerns have been addressed and that they have a clear understanding of your advice.

b. Know Your Audience

Some directors are deep into governance; others care more about financials or operations. Adjust your approach accordingly. Understanding the individual expertise and interests of each board member is crucial for tailoring your communication style and ensuring that your advice resonates with them.

Research Board Members. Research the backgrounds and expertise of each board member to understand their areas of interest.

Tailor Your Presentations. Tailor your presentations to address the specific interests of each board member.

Provide Targeted Information. Provide targeted information that is relevant to their areas of expertise.

Use Language They Understand. Use language that is appropriate for their level of expertise.

b. Be a Steady Presence

If you're only seen when problems arise, you're the bearer of bad news. Stay visible and engaged year-round. Maintaining a consistent presence and proactive engagement with the board throughout the year helps to build trust, foster open communication, and position you as a valuable resource rather than just the bearer of bad news.

Attend Board Committee Meetings. Attend board committee meetings to stay informed of key issues and provide legal guidance.

Provide Regular Updates. Provide regular updates on legal and regulatory developments that could impact the company.
Offer Training Sessions. Offer training sessions on legal and compliance topics to help board members stay informed and engaged.
Participate in Social Events. Participate in social events to build rapport and strengthen relationships with board members.

4. The Fine Art of Board Meeting Prep (And What Not to Say in the Minutes)

Board meetings are high-stakes performances, and preparation is everything. If you're scrambling the night before to finalize materials, you're already behind. Here's how to ensure you walk into the room ready to add value.

a. Control the Narrative

The board agenda is your roadmap. Get ahead of it. Taking control of the narrative in board meetings involves proactive planning, clear communication, and strategic coordination to ensure that legal issues are presented accurately and effectively.

b. Know What's Coming

Coordinate with the CEO, CFO, and corporate secretary to anticipate key discussion points. Collaborating with key stakeholders to anticipate discussion points allows you to prepare thoroughly, gather relevant information, and develop clear recommendations, ensuring that you are well-equipped to address any questions or concerns that may arise during the meeting.
Review the Agenda. Review the board meeting agenda well in advance to identify key discussion points.
Meet with Key Stakeholders. Meet with the CEO, CFO, and corporate secretary to discuss their priorities and concerns.
Anticipate Questions. Anticipate the questions that board members are likely to ask and prepare clear and concise answers.
Gather Supporting Documents. Gather all relevant supporting documents and materials to provide context and support your recommendations.

c. Pre-Brief Where Necessary

If a sensitive legal matter is on the agenda, ensure directors aren't blindsided in the meeting. Pre-briefing directors on sensitive legal matters ensures that they are well-informed, prepared to ask informed questions, and able to engage in constructive discussions during the meeting.

Identify Sensitive Issues. Identify any sensitive legal issues that are likely to be discussed at the meeting.

Prepare Pre-Briefing Materials. Prepare pre-briefing materials that provide context, background information, and key talking points.

Schedule One-on-One Meetings. Schedule one-on-one meetings with directors to discuss any sensitive legal issues in advance of the meeting.

Address Concerns. Address any concerns or questions that directors may have and provide them with the information they need to make informed decisions.

d. Be Clear and Concise in Materials

No 50-page memos. Stick to high-impact summaries with actionable takeaways. Providing clear and concise materials ensures that board members can quickly grasp the key issues, understand the potential risks and rewards, and make informed decisions without being overwhelmed by excessive detail.

Use Executive Summaries. Use executive summaries to highlight the key points of each document.

Focus on Actionable Takeaways. Focus on providing actionable takeaways that the board can use to make informed decisions.

Use Visual Aids. Use visual aids, such as charts and graphs, to illustrate complex information.

Keep it Brief. Keep your materials as brief as possible, focusing on the most important information.

5. Steer Clear of Landmines in the Minutes

Minutes are a legal record. What's written can (and will) be scrutinized in litigation or regulatory investigations. Avoid these common pitfalls:

a. No Unnecessary Detail

The minutes should reflect what was decided, not every discussion point. Focusing on the decisions made and the rationale behind them, rather than every detail of the discussion, ensures that the minutes are clear, concise, and legally sound.

Focus on Decisions. Focus on documenting the decisions made by the board, rather than every detail of the discussion.

Summarize Discussions. Summarize the key points of the discussions, rather than transcribing them verbatim.

Avoid Personal Opinions. Avoid including personal opinions or subjective statements in the minutes.

Use Clear and Concise Language. Use clear and concise language to describe the decisions made and the rationale behind them.

b. 5.2 Avoid Subjective or Speculative Language

Phrases like "The board was deeply concerned" or "It was unclear whether management had a firm plan" can be used against you. Avoiding subjective or speculative language ensures that the minutes remain objective, factual, and legally defensible.

Use Objective Language. Use objective language to describe the discussions and decisions made by the board.

Avoid Speculative Statements. Avoid making speculative statements about the future or the potential outcomes of certain actions.

Focus on Facts. Focus on documenting the facts and avoid drawing conclusions or making interpretations.

Review Carefully. Review the minutes carefully to ensure that they do not contain any subjective or speculative language.

c. Document Key Approvals and Dissent

If a director objects to a decision, note that they dissented—but don't go into unnecessary commentary. Documenting key approvals and dissent ensures that the minutes accurately reflect the board's decision-making process and protect the company from potential liability.

Document All Approvals. Document all approvals made by the board, including the date, time, and vote count.

Note Dissenting Opinions. Note any dissenting opinions expressed by board members, including the name of the dissenting director and a summary of their reasons for dissenting.

Avoid Unnecessary Commentary. Avoid including unnecessary commentary or explanations of the dissenting opinions.

Maintain Accuracy. Ensure that the minutes accurately reflect the board's decision-making process and the views of all board members.

6. Navigating Director Independence, Conflicts of Interest, and Executive Sessions

A well-functioning board isn't just about strategy; it's about governance. And governance gets messy when independence, conflicts, and closed-door sessions come into play.

a. Understanding Director Independence (and Why It's a Constant Battle)

Independent directors are supposed to bring objectivity to board decisions. But true independence can be tricky. Maintaining director independence is crucial for ensuring objective decision-making, protecting shareholder interests, and upholding corporate governance standards.

Define Independence Criteria. Clearly define what constitutes "independence" for directors, considering regulatory standards and best practices.

Evaluate Personal and Financial Ties. Regularly evaluate directors' personal and financial relationships with the company, its executives, and major shareholders.

Scrutinize Tenure and Familiarity. Assess whether long board tenure or close personal connections might compromise a director's objectivity.

Encourage Open Dialogue. Foster a board culture that encourages directors to voice dissenting views and challenge management when necessary.

Rotate Committee Assignments. Periodically rotate directors through different board committees to prevent entrenched interests and promote fresh perspectives.

Document Independence Assessments. Maintain thorough records of independence evaluations and revisit them as circumstances change.

b. Watch for Creeping Conflicts

A director who serves on multiple boards or has past business ties to the CEO may not be as independent as they seem. Monitoring for creeping conflicts involves ongoing vigilance to identify potential threats to director independence and ensure that board members remain objective and impartial.

Review Director Disclosures. Review director disclosures regularly to identify any potential conflicts of interest.

Monitor Outside Activities. Monitor the outside activities of the directors, such as service on other boards or business relationships with the company, to identify potential conflicts.

Assess Relationships with Management. Assess directors' relationships with management to ensure that they are not unduly influenced by the CEO or other executives.

Be Alert to Subtle Conflicts. Be alert to subtle conflicts of interest that may not be immediately apparent.

c. Be Mindful of Informal Alliances

Directors who always side with management may be more beholden than their title suggests. Recognizing and addressing informal alliances is essential for fostering a culture of independent thought and ensuring that all board members have the opportunity to express their views without fear of reprisal.

Observe Board Dynamics. Observe board dynamics to identify any patterns of alignment between directors and management.

Encourage Independent Thought. Encourage directors to express their own views and challenge management's assumptions.

Provide Opportunities for Independent Discussion. Provide opportunities for directors to meet privately without management present.

Be Alert to Groupthink. Be alert to the dangers of groupthink and encourage directors to consider alternative perspectives.

d. Regulators Are Paying Attention

The SEC and investors scrutinize independence. Stay ahead of any red flags. Staying ahead of regulatory scrutiny regarding director independence requires proactive monitoring, robust disclosure practices, and a commitment to upholding the highest standards of corporate governance.

Stay Informed of Regulatory Requirements. Stay informed of the latest regulatory requirements regarding director independence.

Ensure Accurate Disclosures. Ensure that the company's disclosures regarding director independence are accurate and complete.

Monitor Investor Sentiment. Monitor investor sentiment regarding director independence and address any concerns that may arise.

Be Prepared to Defend Independence. Be prepared to defend the company's director independence practices to regulators and investors.

7. Managing Conflicts of Interest Without Drama

Conflicts happen. How they're handled determines whether they become a problem. Managing conflicts of interest effectively requires transparency, proactive disclosure, and a commitment to upholding the highest standards of ethical conduct.

a. Require Proactive Disclosure

Directors should regularly disclose financial and personal ties that could influence decision-making. Requiring proactive disclosure of potential conflicts ensures that the board is aware of any relationships or interests that could influence a director's decision-making and allows them to take appropriate action to mitigate any potential risks.

Implement a Conflict-of-Interest Policy. Implement a conflict-of-interest policy that requires directors to disclose any financial or personal ties that could influence their decision-making.

Provide Disclosure Forms. Provide directors with disclosure forms that are easy to understand and complete.

Review Disclosures Regularly. Review director disclosures regularly to identify any potential conflicts of interest.

Update Disclosures as Needed. Require directors to update their disclosures as needed to reflect any changes in their financial or personal ties.

b. Recusal Isn't Always Enough

If a director has a material conflict, stepping out of one discussion may not suffice—they may need to step off the board. Recognizing when recusal is insufficient and taking appropriate action, such as requesting a director to step down from the board, is essential for protecting the company's interests and maintaining the integrity of its decision-making process.

Assess the Materiality of the Conflict. Assess the materiality of the conflict to determine whether recusal is sufficient to protect the company's interests.

Consider the Director's Influence. Consider the director's influence on the board and the potential impact of their conflict on decision-making.

Seek Legal Advice. Seek legal advice to determine the appropriate course of action.

Be Prepared to Request Resignation. Be prepared to request the director's resignation if the conflict is material and cannot be effectively managed through recusal.

c. Transparency Is Your Best Defense

When conflicts arise, document how they were addressed in a way that withstands scrutiny. Maintaining transparency in addressing conflicts of interest demonstrates a commitment to ethical conduct, protects the company from potential liability, and builds trust with stakeholders.

Document All Conflicts. Document all conflicts of interest that arise, including the nature of the conflict, the steps taken to address it, and the rationale behind the decision made.

Maintain Detailed Minutes. Maintain detailed minutes of board meetings that accurately reflect the discussions and decisions made regarding conflicts of interest.

Disclose Conflicts in Proxy Statements. Disclose any material conflicts of interest in the company's proxy statements.

Seek Legal Review. Seek legal review of the company's conflict-of-interest policies and procedures to ensure that they comply with applicable laws and regulations.

8. Making the Most of Executive Sessions

Executive sessions—where independent directors meet without management—can be a GC's best friend or worst nightmare. Utilizing executive sessions effectively requires understanding their purpose, fostering open communication, and ensuring that any concerns raised are addressed promptly and appropriately.

a. Know When You're Needed

If legal matters are discussed, you may be asked to join part of the session. Understanding when your presence is required in executive sessions allows you to provide timely legal guidance, address any legal concerns that may arise, and ensure that the board's discussions are informed by accurate and up-to-date legal information.

Stay Informed of the Agenda. Stay informed of the agenda for executive sessions to anticipate any legal matters that may be discussed.

Communicate with the Lead Independent Director. Communicate with the lead independent director to determine whether your presence is required.

Be Prepared to Provide Guidance. Be prepared to provide legal guidance on any legal matters that may be discussed during the session.

Respect Confidentiality. Respect the confidentiality of the discussions that take place during the executive session.

b. Gauge Director Concerns

What's said in these meetings often signals broader board sentiment. Gauging directors' concerns expressed during executive sessions provides valuable insights into the board's overall sentiment, allowing you to proactively address any issues that may be brewing and ensure that the board's concerns are taken seriously.

Seek Feedback from Directors. Seek feedback from directors after executive sessions to understand their concerns and priorities.
Observe Non-Verbal Cues. Observe directors' non-verbal cues during board meetings and executive sessions to gauge their level of engagement and concern.
Identify Emerging Issues. Identify any emerging issues that are being discussed in executive sessions and take steps to address them proactively.
Communicate with Management. Communicate any concerns raised by directors during executive sessions to management and work together to develop solutions.

c. Keep an Open Line of Communication

If directors have concerns about management, they should feel comfortable bringing them to you. Maintaining open communication with directors ensures that they feel comfortable sharing their concerns, allows you to address any issues promptly and effectively, and fosters a culture of trust and transparency within the board.

Establish Rapport. Establish a rapport with directors based on trust and mutual respect.
Be Accessible. Be accessible to directors and make yourself available to answer their questions and address their concerns.
Listen Actively. Listen actively to directors' concerns and demonstrate that you are taking their feedback seriously.
Follow Up Promptly. Follow up promptly on any concerns raised by directors and provide them with timely updates.

9. Understanding Board Dynamics and Director Personalities

The Board is a collection of individuals with varying backgrounds, experiences, and personalities. Understanding the dynamics at play and the traits of each director is crucial for effective communication and influence.

a. Identifying Board Archetypes

The Visionary. Focused on long-term strategy and innovation.

The Financier. Obsessed with financial performance and shareholder value.

The Operator. Experienced in day-to-day management and execution.

The Governance Expert. Deeply knowledgeable about corporate governance and compliance.

The Diplomat. Skilled at building consensus and resolving conflicts.

The Contrarian. Challenges assumptions and asks tough questions.

b. Adapting Your Communication Style

The Visionary. Present innovative solutions and strategic insights.

The Financier. Provide data-driven analysis and quantify the financial impact of legal decisions.

The Operator. Focus on practical implementation and operational efficiency.

The Governance Expert. Emphasize compliance and risk management.

The Diplomat. Build consensus and find common ground.

The Contrarian. Be prepared to defend your position and challenge assumptions.

c. Building Relationships with Different Personalities

The Visionary. Share your long-term vision for the company and its legal strategy.

The Financier. Demonstrate your understanding of financial performance and shareholder value.

The Operator. Show your ability to execute and deliver results.

The Governance Expert. Demonstrate your knowledge of corporate governance and compliance.

The Diplomat. Be a good listener and build consensus.

The Contrarian. Respect their perspective and be prepared to engage in thoughtful debate.

10. The Evolving Corporate Governance Landscape and Emerging Challenges

The corporate governance landscape is constantly evolving, presenting new challenges and opportunities for boards of directors. Staying informed of these developments and adapting governance practices accordingly is essential for long-term success.

a. Key Trends in Corporate Governance

ESG (Environmental, Social, and Governance) Factors. Investors are increasingly focused on ESG factors and their impact on long-term value creation.

Cybersecurity and Data Privacy. Boards are responsible for overseeing the company's cybersecurity and data privacy practices.

Diversity and Inclusion. Boards are under pressure to increase diversity and inclusion at all levels of the organization.

Activist Investors. Activist investors are becoming more sophisticated and assertive in their demands for change.

Executive Compensation. Executive compensation is a perennial hot topic, and boards must ensure that pay practices are aligned with performance and shareholder interests.

b. Addressing Emerging Challenges

ESG. Integrate ESG factors into the company's strategic planning and risk management processes.

Cybersecurity. Implement robust cybersecurity policies and procedures and provide regular training to employees.

Diversity and Inclusion. Develop a comprehensive diversity and inclusion strategy and set measurable goals.

Activist Investors. Engage with activist investors constructively and be prepared to defend the company's strategy and performance.

Executive Compensation. Review executive compensation practices regularly to ensure that they are aligned with performance and shareholder interests.

Five-Point Framework for the General Counsel to Work Effectively with the Board

1. Communicate with Clarity, Business Focus, and Brevity
- Speak in plain, business-oriented language—avoid legal jargon and translate legal risks into business consequences, financial terms, and strategic impacts.
- Use concise executive summaries, elevator pitches, and visual aids to ensure directors quickly grasp the core issues and recommended actions.
- Quantify risks and opportunities wherever possible, providing concrete data (e.g., potential fines, ROI, historical precedents) to support decision-making.

2. Be a Balanced, Solution-Oriented Advisor
- Provide objective, prioritized risk assessments—distinguish between critical and routine issues using tools like risk matrices.
- Always offer actionable solutions, not just problems, and tailor recommendations to align with business objectives and the company's risk tolerance.
- Balance legal caution with pragmatic advice, enabling the board to make informed decisions without undue alarmism or paralysis.

3. Build Trust Through Proactive, Personalized Engagement
- Develop relationships beyond formal meetings by engaging directors one-on-one, understanding their individual concerns, and tailoring advice accordingly.
- Maintain a consistent, visible presence throughout the year (not just in crises), provide regular updates, attend committee meetings, and offer training sessions.
- Adapt communication style and content to the varied backgrounds and interests of individual directors and board archetypes (e.g., Visionary, Financier, Operator).

4. Master Board Meeting Preparation and Documentation

- Take control of the meeting narrative by preparing thoroughly: coordinate with key executives, anticipate questions, and pre-brief directors on sensitive issues.
- Ensure board materials are clear, concise, and actionable; prioritize executive summaries and visual aids over lengthy memos.
- Guide the minute-taking process: document decisions and rationale, avoid unnecessary detail or subjective language, and accurately record dissent without commentary.

5. Uphold Governance Integrity: Independence, Conflicts, and Executive Sessions

- Monitor and manage director independence and conflicts of interest proactively, requiring regular disclosures and addressing material conflicts decisively (recusal or resignation if needed).
- Facilitate effective executive sessions by knowing when to participate, maintaining confidentiality, and ensuring directors' concerns are heard and addressed.
- Stay ahead of regulatory expectations, document conflict management transparently, and foster a culture of open communication and ethical governance.

Case Studies

Scenario I: Navigating Board Tensions After a Strategic Setback
A General Counsel at a mid-sized technology company notices increasing tension among board members following a failed product launch. In the last board meeting, several directors voiced concerns about risk oversight and questioned whether management had provided enough information for sound decision-making. The atmosphere was tense, with some directors focusing on governance failures, while others were more concerned about financial impacts or operational missteps. The GC recognizes that trust is eroding, and communication is faltering—not just in formal meetings, but also in the crucial informal interactions where relationships are built.

How the General Counsel Should Handle This Situation

Engage with Directors One-on-One
- The GC should schedule individual meetings with each director, using these sessions to listen actively to their unique concerns and perspectives. For example, the GC might discover that one director is particularly worried about regulatory exposure, while another is focused on reputational risk or operational resilience.
- By asking clarifying questions and demonstrating genuine interest, the GC can tailor legal advice and risk mitigation strategies to each director's priorities, ensuring they feel heard and valued.

Know Your Audience
- Before each one-on-one meeting, the GC should research the director's background, board committee roles, and professional expertise. This preparation allows the GC to use language and examples that resonate with each individual, discussing compliance frameworks with governance-focused directors, and financial risk controls with those more attuned to the bottom line.
- Tailoring presentations and communications in this way ensures that advice is relevant and actionable for each board member.

Be a Steady Presence
- The GC should maintain visibility outside of crisis moments by regularly attending committee meetings, offering proactive legal updates, and participating in board social events. This positions the GC as a resource and partner, not just a messenger of bad news.

- Offering short training sessions on emerging legal or regulatory issues can further demonstrate commitment to the board's ongoing education and engagement.

Follow Up and Build Trust
- After each meeting or conversation, the GC should follow up with a concise summary, addressing any outstanding questions and providing additional resources as needed. This reinforces the GC's reliability and responsiveness.
- The GC should also provide regular, transparent updates to the entire board about legal and regulatory developments, ensuring there are no surprises and that all directors feel informed and included.

Foster Open, Honest Communication
- The GC should model transparency by sharing both challenges and successes, and by inviting directors to raise concerns early. This approach builds credibility and encourages a culture where issues are surfaced and addressed collaboratively, rather than festering in silence.
- By consistently demonstrating integrity and ethical judgment, the GC helps rebuild trust not just between management and the board, but among directors themselves.

Key Takeaways

In the wake of a failed product launch and growing boardroom tensions, the General Counsel plays a pivotal role in restoring trust and strengthening governance by engaging directors individually, tailoring advice to their unique concerns, and maintaining a visible, steady presence both in and outside formal meetings. By preparing thoroughly for each interaction, following up with clear and responsive communication, and fostering a culture of transparency and open dialogue, the GC not only addresses immediate risk and governance issues but also rebuilds the informal relationships essential for effective board dynamics. Through these deliberate actions, the GC helps bridge divides, ensures directors feel informed and valued, and lays the groundwork for a more resilient and collaborative board moving forward.

Scenario II: Board Minutes Landmine

The board of directors of Acme Corp. convenes to discuss a major restructuring proposal. During the meeting, several directors express strong reservations about the CEO's plan, citing concerns about potential layoffs and the lack of a detailed risk mitigation strategy. One director, Ms. Smith, is particularly vocal, stating, "I am deeply concerned that this plan could backfire and damage our reputation." After a lengthy debate, the board votes 7-2 in favor of the restructuring, with Ms. Smith and Mr. Lee dissenting.

The draft minutes, prepared by the board secretary, include the following passage:

Several directors expressed deep concern about the CEO's proposal, questioning whether management had a firm plan for addressing potential layoffs. Ms. Smith stated she was 'deeply concerned' about reputational damage. After extensive debate, the board approved the restructuring plan, with Ms. Smith and Mr. Lee dissenting.

How the General Counsel Should Handle the Scenario

1. Identify and Address Landmines

The general counsel should recognize that the draft minutes contain several pitfalls:

Unnecessary Detail & Subjective Language. The minutes record individual directors' emotional responses ("deep concern") and speculative statements about management's preparedness ("questioning whether management had a firm plan"), both of which can be problematic if the minutes are scrutinized in litigation or regulatory investigations.

Personal Opinions. The verbatim quote from Ms. Smith introduces personal opinion, which should be avoided in official minutes.

2. Advise Revision for Objectivity and Brevity

The general counsel should instruct the secretary to revise the minutes to focus on the decisions made, the rationale, and any dissent, without unnecessary detail or subjective commentary. For example, the revised minutes might read:

"The board discussed the proposed restructuring plan, including considerations regarding workforce impacts and risk mitigation. After discussion, the board approved the plan by a vote of 7-2. Directors Smith and Lee dissented."

Remove Subjective and Speculative Language. Eliminate phrases like "deep concern" and "questioning whether management had a firm plan," as these are subjective and could be used to challenge the board's process or diligence in future disputes.

Summarize, Don't Transcribe. Ensure that the minutes summarize the key points of discussion and the rationale for the decision, not every detail or personal statement.

Document Dissent Properly. Clearly record the dissenting votes, including the directors' names, but avoid unnecessary commentary or detailed explanations of their objections.

Review and Approve. The general counsel should review the revised draft to confirm it is objective, factual, and free of personal opinions or speculative language before it is finalized and entered into the corporate record.

Key Takeaways

The General Counsel plays a critical role in safeguarding Acme Corp.'s interests by ensuring that board minutes are objective, concise, and free from subjective or speculative language. The initial draft minutes present significant risks by including emotional statements and personal opinions, which could be problematic if scrutinized during litigation or regulatory reviews. To mitigate these risks, the general counsel should guide the revision process so that the minutes accurately reflect the board's actions, the general rationale for the decision, and the record of dissent, without attributing personal sentiments or verbatim quotes to individual directors. This approach not only strengthens the integrity of the corporate record but also protects the board and the company from potential future challenges related to the decision-making process.

Scenario III: Navigating Director Independence, Conflicts of Interest, and Executive Sessions

The board of XYZ Corporation is preparing to vote on the proposed acquisition of a smaller competitor. One independent director, Ms. Lee, has recently joined the board. She also sits on the board of a supplier to XYZ and previously worked with XYZ's CEO at another company. Another director, Mr. Patel, is known to consistently support management's proposals and rarely challenges the CEO. The board is scheduled to discuss the acquisition in an upcoming meeting, with an executive session to follow. Ms. Lee's outside board role and prior relationship with the CEO may compromise her independence, even if she technically meets NYSE standards. Mr. Patel's pattern of siding with management raises concerns about informal alliances and potential groupthink. Ms. Lee's position with a supplier creates a potential conflict of interest regarding the acquisition, as the supplier could benefit from the transaction. The board plans to hold an executive session (without management present) to discuss the acquisition and any concerns about director independence or conflicts.

How the General Counsel Should Handle This Scenario

1. Proactively Review Director Disclosures and Relationships
The general counsel (GC) should review all director disclosures, focusing on Ms. Lee's outside board service and prior relationship with the CEO. The GC should assess whether these relationships constitute a material relationship that could impair her independence, referencing NYSE and company-specific standards.

2. Identify and Manage Conflicts of Interest
  • The GC should ensure Ms. Lee fully discloses her supplier board role and any potential impact on the acquisition.
  • Following best practices, Ms. Lee should recuse herself from discussions and voting on the acquisition if a conflict is determined.
  • If multiple directors are conflicted, the GC should recommend forming an independent committee to evaluate the transaction or, if necessary, seek shareholder approval with full disclosure.

3. Monitor for Informal Alliances and Groupthink
  • The GC should observe board dynamics, noting Mr. Patel's consistent alignment with management.

- The GC can encourage the board chair to foster independent thought *by soliciting diverse perspectives and challenging assumptions.*

4. Facilitate Effective Executive Sessions
- The GC should help the board establish or follow a formal executive session policy, clarifying the purpose and process for these meetings.
- The GC may serve as custodian of executive session minutes, ensuring confidentiality and proper documentation.
- After the session, the GC or board chair should communicate any conclusions or recommendations to the CEO, maintaining transparency without breaching confidentiality.

5. Ensure Regulatory Compliance and Robust Disclosure
- The GC must ensure all independence and conflict disclosures are accurate, complete, and up to date in public filings, anticipating potential SEC or investor scrutiny.
- The GC should stay informed of evolving regulatory requirements and be prepared to defend the company's practices to regulators and investors if challenged.

Key Takeaways

In navigating the complexities of director independence, conflicts of interest, and executive sessions surrounding XYZ Corporation's proposed acquisition, the general counsel plays a pivotal role in safeguarding board integrity and regulatory compliance. By proactively scrutinizing director disclosures—particularly Ms. Lee's supplier board role and prior CEO relationship—and ensuring full transparency, the GC helps identify and mitigate potential conflicts that could compromise objective decision-making. Encouraging recusal where appropriate, monitoring for informal alliances such as Mr. Patel's consistent alignment with management, and fostering a culture of independent thought are essential steps to prevent groupthink and uphold fiduciary duties. Facilitating well-structured executive sessions and maintaining rigorous documentation further support effective governance, while robust, up-to-date public disclosures help anticipate regulatory scrutiny. Through these measures, the GC not only protects the company's interests but also reinforces the board's credibility and trustworthiness in the eyes of shareholders and regulators.

Final Thought: The Board's Trust is Earned, Not Assumed
Surviving and thriving in the boardroom isn't about knowing every regulation; it's about being the person whom directors trust to guide them through uncertainty. Build credibility, stay ahead of governance issues, understand board dynamics and director personalities, and ensure board meetings run smoothly. Do that, and you won't just survive, you'll thrive.

FIVE

THE LEGAL DEPARTMENT

–

BUILDING A DREAM TEAM THAT WON'T BURN OUT

The Legal Department—Building a Dream Team That Won't Burn Out

A truly exceptional legal team is much more than just a cost center; it's a strategic asset that can significantly impact an organization's success. When built and managed effectively, a legal team acts as a force multiplier, not only safeguarding the company from legal risks and liabilities but also proactively enabling business growth and innovation. A well-functioning legal department provides invaluable guidance on regulatory compliance, intellectual property protection, contract negotiation, and risk management, allowing the company to operate confidently and pursue its strategic objectives without undue legal impediments.

Conversely, a poorly constructed or mismanaged legal team can become a significant drain on resources, a source of constant crises, and a major impediment to business progress. A reactive, firefighting legal team spends its time addressing problems after they arise, rather than anticipating and preventing them. This can lead to costly litigation, regulatory penalties, reputational damage, and missed business opportunities. Perhaps the most detrimental consequence of a dysfunctional legal team is the premature departure of talented lawyers due to burnout, high stress levels, and a lack of opportunities for professional growth. Replacing these lawyers can be expensive and time-consuming, and it can disrupt the continuity of legal services and institutional knowledge.

Building a robust legal team transcends the simple act of hiring intelligent and qualified lawyers. It necessitates carefully assembling a group of professionals who possess the right combination of specialized legal skills, sharp business acumen, exceptional communication abilities, and a high degree of adaptability to navigate the ever-changing legal and business landscape. It also requires adeptly managing diverse personalities, fluctuating workloads, and often unrealistic expectations from various stakeholders within the organization. Critically, it involves cultivating a supportive and empowering environment where team members can perform at a consistently high level without succumbing to the pressures of overwork, stress, and a lack of work-life balance.

Let's delve deeper into the essential elements of constructing a legal team that not only endures the challenges it faces but actively thrives, contributes significantly to the overall success of the organization, and fosters a culture of collaboration, innovation, and professional growth.

The Must-Have Skill Sets for Your Legal Team

When staffing a legal department, many organizations tend to prioritize legal expertise and technical proficiency above all else. While a deep understanding of the law is undoubtedly a fundamental requirement, it's no longer sufficient to have lawyers who simply provide answers to specific legal questions or interpret existing laws and regulations. In today's complex and rapidly evolving business environment, you need individuals who can anticipate potential legal and regulatory issues and proactively develop strategies to mitigate them before they escalate into significant problems that could harm the organization. A legal team that actively aligns itself with the overarching business strategy of the company and proactively identifies potential legal hurdles and opportunities is far more valuable than one that merely reacts to crises and legal challenges as they arise. You need:

Strategic Thinkers
Strategic thinking in a legal context involves a comprehensive understanding of the long-term implications of legal decisions and how those decisions

directly impact the company's overall strategic objectives. It requires the ability to see beyond the immediate legal issue and consider the broader business context, including market trends, competitive pressures, and emerging technologies. Strategic legal thinkers can anticipate future legal challenges and develop proactive strategies to address them, such as lobbying for favorable legislation, developing compliance programs, or negotiating favorable contracts.

Business-Savvy Advisors

A truly effective legal team must possess a deep understanding of the company's specific industry, its underlying business model, its competitive landscape, and its overall tolerance for risk. Without this essential business acumen, legal advice can be either overly cautious, which can stifle innovation, slow down business progress, and prevent the company from capitalizing on emerging opportunities, or excessively aggressive, which can expose the company to unnecessary and potentially damaging legal risks, financial penalties, and reputational harm.

Business acumen for a lawyer means understanding fundamental financial statements, analyzing key performance indicators (KPIs), identifying critical market trends, assessing the competitive landscape, and understanding the key drivers of profitability and value creation within the company's specific industry. It also involves being able to communicate complex legal advice in a clear, concise, and persuasive manner that is relevant and easily understandable to non-legal professionals, such as executives, business managers, and sales representatives.

A business-savvy lawyer combines legal expertise with commercial insight, ensuring legal strategy is a proactive driver of business growth and resilience.

Crisis Managers

Every company, regardless of its size, industry, or geographic location, will inevitably face crises and unexpected challenges at some point in its existence. These crises can take various forms, including high-stakes litigation, formal regulatory investigations, damaging data breaches and cybersecurity incidents, product recalls, environmental disasters, or significant public relations crises that threaten the company's reputation. In such high-pressure situations, the legal team must be exceptionally well-equipped to respond calmly, decisively, and strategically, providing timely and effective guidance to protect the company's interests and mitigate potential damage.

Effective crisis management requires a pre-defined and well-documented plan that clearly outlines roles, responsibilities, and communication protocols for the legal team and other key stakeholders within the organization. It also involves the ability to quickly gather accurate information, thoroughly assess the situation, identify potential legal risks, and develop a coordinated and comprehensive response strategy that addresses all relevant legal, regulatory, and public relations considerations.

Excellent Communicators

Lawyers are often perceived as speaking their own unique and highly specialized language filled with complex legal jargon, technical terms, and convoluted sentence structures. However, the most effective legal teams are able to translate these complex legal concepts, intricate terminology, and often arcane legal principles into plain, easily understandable English that can be readily grasped by non-legal professionals. If the executive team, the board of directors, or other critical stakeholders within the organization cannot clearly understand the legal risks associated with a particular business decision or strategic initiative, they may make uninformed or ill-advised choices that could expose the company to significant legal liabilities or, even worse, completely disregard the legal advice being provided by the legal team.

Excellent communication skills encompass a wide range of abilities, including the ability to write clearly, concisely, and persuasively, present complex information effectively in a variety of formats (such as oral presentations, written reports, and visual aids), actively listen to and understand the concerns of others, and tailor your communication style to the specific needs and expectations of your audience. It also involves being able to explain complex legal concepts in a simple and accessible manner, avoiding unnecessary jargon and technical terms.

By proactively communicating legal risks, aligning compliance with business strategy, and supporting implementation, in-house counsel helps ensure the successful and responsible execution of high-stakes corporate initiatives.

Negotiation & Relationship Builders

Your legal team will interact with a wide and diverse range of individuals and entities, including government regulators, external legal counsel and expert witnesses, internal business units and functional departments, and, in some cases, potentially hostile counterparties in litigation or contractual disputes. To navigate these often complex and challenging interactions effectively, they must possess strong negotiation skills, excellent interpersonal abilities, and the ability to build and maintain positive, mutually beneficial relationships with a wide variety of stakeholders.

Negotiation skills involve the ability to understand the other party's underlying interests, identify areas of common ground and potential compromise, and develop creative solutions that meet both parties' needs and objectives. It also requires the ability to remain calm and professional under pressure, manage conflict constructively, and know when to walk away from a deal that is not in the company's best interests or that poses unacceptable risks.

An in-house lawyer with strong negotiation and relationship-building skills strategically prepares, builds trust, gathers intelligence, negotiates effectively, finds creative solutions, and maintains professionalism to achieve optimal outcomes while safeguarding future business relationships.

How to Hire (and Fire) Effectively

The process of hiring top-tier legal talent can be exceptionally complex and challenging, particularly in a competitive market for skilled lawyers. The most talented and highly sought-after lawyers are not solely motivated by financial compensation; they are also seeking meaningful and intellectually stimulating work, a positive and supportive work culture that values collaboration and work-life balance, and leadership they can trust, respect, and learn from. Here's a comprehensive guide to hiring effectively and, when necessary and unavoidable, making the difficult but essential decision to terminate an employee who is not performing adequately or is not a good fit for the team.

Hire for Judgment, Not Just Experience

While a stellar resume filled with impressive credentials, accolades, and experience at prestigious law firms or corporations may be initially tempting and appealing, a lawyer with poor judgment, a lack of ethical compass, or a questionable decision-making process can be a significant liability to the organization, potentially exposing the company to legal risks, financial penalties, and reputational damage. It's crucial to seek out candidates who demonstrate the ability to make sound and well-reasoned decisions under pressure, adapt quickly and effectively to new and evolving challenges, and strike a delicate balance between mitigating potential legal risks and supporting the company's overall business objectives.

> **Interview Tip.** Instead of simply asking candidates about their past experiences and focusing solely on their technical legal skills, present them with a hypothetical crisis scenario or a complex legal dilemma that requires them to exercise their judgment and critical thinking abilities. Observe carefully how they approach the problem, the factors they consider in their analysis, the alternative solutions they propose, and the rationale behind their ultimate recommendations. This will provide valuable insights into their judgment, decision-making process, and ability to think strategically under pressure. For example, you could ask them how they would handle a situation where the company is facing a potential data breach involving sensitive customer information or a lawsuit from a disgruntled employee alleging discrimination or wrongful termination.

Assess Cultural Fit

It is essential that the members of your legal team align closely with the company's core values, its overall culture, its preferred working style, and its appetite for risk. A highly conservative and risk-averse lawyer working in a fast-paced, innovative, and high-growth startup environment will likely clash with the company's entrepreneurial spirit, its willingness to take calculated risks, and its emphasis on speed and agility. Similarly, an overly aggressive, risk-taking, and compliance-averse lawyer in a heavily regulated industry, such as financial services or healthcare, could expose the company to significant compliance violations, regulatory scrutiny, financial penalties, and potential reputational damage.

> **Interview Tip.** Beyond evaluating a candidate's legal expertise, incorporate behavioral and situational questions that reveal how they align with the company's values and preferred ways of working. For example, ask the candidate to describe a time when they had to advocate for a position that was unpopular with business leaders or when they had to balance legal risk with business objectives. Pay close attention to how they navigated the tension between legal compliance and business needs, the stakeholders they involved, and how they communicated their recommendations.

Intellectual Curiosity and Willingness to Learn

Lawyers who are intellectually curious ask probing questions, seek to understand the "why" behind issues, and are open to new ideas. This curiosity drives them to stay current with changes in law and business, adapt to evolving company needs, and proactively identify risks and opportunities. Such lawyers are more likely to become trusted advisors, not just technical experts.

> **Interview Tip.** To assess a candidate's intellectual curiosity and willingness to learn, go beyond asking about what they already know. Present them with a recent legal development or a new area of law that is relevant to your industry but may be outside their direct experience. Ask them how they would go about understanding the issue, what resources they would use, and how they would ensure they stay current as the law evolves. Pay close attention to whether they demonstrate an eagerness to explore unfamiliar topics, their approach to self-education, and their openness to seeking input from others.

Flexibility and Adaptability

The needs of a legal department can shift rapidly as the business evolves. Lawyers who demonstrate flexibility—those who can take on new roles, adjust to changing priorities, and thrive in ambiguity—are invaluable. Look for candidates who have taken on varied responsibilities in previous roles and who show a willingness to "play different positions on the team."

> **Interview Tip.** To evaluate a candidate's flexibility and adaptability, move beyond general questions and present them with a real-world scenario that reflects the unpredictable nature of the legal and business environment. For example, describe a situation where priorities shift suddenly or a project changes direction midstream, and ask the candidate how they would respond and adapt their approach. Pay close attention to their problem-solving process, willingness to embrace change, and ability to remain composed under pressure.

Strong Communication Skills

Effective legal professionals must be able to communicate complex legal concepts clearly and persuasively, both in writing and verbally. This skill is critical not only for drafting documents and negotiating agreements, but also for collaborating with business partners and explaining legal risks in accessible terms.

> **Interview Tip.** To effectively evaluate a candidate's communication skills, prompt them to describe a specific instance where they had to explain a complex legal concept to a non-legal audience, such as business partners or clients. Listen for their ability to break down legal jargon, tailor their message to the audience, and ensure understanding through clear, concise, and persuasive language.

Teamwork and Collaboration

Legal work is rarely done in isolation. Lawyers must be able to collaborate effectively with colleagues, business units, and external partners. The ability to work well in teams enhances knowledge sharing, improves legal strategies, and fosters a positive work environment.

Interview Tip. To effectively assess a candidate's teamwork and collaboration skills—especially crucial in legal work where cross-functional cooperation is the norm—ask behavioral interview questions that require the candidate to provide specific examples from their past experience. Frame your question to prompt a STAR (Situation, Task, Action, Result) response, which ensures the candidate details not just what happened, but their role, actions, and the outcome.

Empathy and Emotional Intelligence

Empathy allows lawyers to better understand the perspectives and needs of their clients, colleagues, and other stakeholders. High emotional intelligence helps them navigate complex interpersonal dynamics, build trust, and manage conflict constructively.

Interview Tip. To effectively assess empathy and emotional intelligence in legal candidates, go beyond technical or knowledge-based questions. Instead, incorporate behavioral and situational interview questions that require candidates to demonstrate their ability to understand and manage emotions—both their own and those of others.

Professional Ethics and Integrity

A strong ethical foundation is non-negotiable. Lawyers must consistently demonstrate honesty, integrity, and respect for professional rules. This not only protects the company's reputation but also builds trust with internal and external stakeholders.

Interview Tip. To effectively evaluate a legal candidate's ethics and integrity, go beyond theoretical knowledge or recitation of professional rules. Instead, ask behavioral interview questions that require the candidate to describe specific past experiences where their ethical standards were tested.

Initiative and Proactivity

The best lawyers don't just react to problems—they anticipate them. Look for candidates who show initiative, seek out opportunities for improvement, and take ownership of their work. Proactive lawyers help the business stay ahead of legal risks and seize new opportunities.

Interview Tip. When interviewing candidates for legal roles where initiative and proactivity are critical, don't just settle for generic claims of being a "self-starter." Instead, ask candidates to describe a specific situation where they anticipated a legal or business risk before it became an issue and took concrete steps to address it without being prompted.

Attention to Detail

Legal work often hinges on the smallest details. Lawyers who are meticulous and thorough are less likely to make costly mistakes and more likely to produce high-quality work that stands up to scrutiny.

Interview Tip. When interviewing candidates for legal roles where attention to detail is critical, go beyond generic questions. Ask candidates to describe a time when their meticulousness prevented a significant error or led to a better outcome.

Strong Work Ethic

A commitment to excellence, reliability under pressure, and willingness to go the extra mile are essential in the demanding environment of a corporate legal department.

Interview Tip. Prompt candidates to share concrete examples that demonstrate their commitment to excellence, reliability under pressure, and willingness to go the extra mile.

Fire Fast When Necessary

A poor hiring decision within the legal department can have serious and far-reaching consequences for the organization, potentially leading to legal errors, compliance violations, ethical breaches, and damage to the company's reputation. If an individual is demonstrably not a good fit for the team, whether due to poor judgment, a consistently negative attitude, an inability to effectively manage their workload, a lack of commitment to the company's values, or an inability to keep up with the evolving demands of the role, it is important to take swift and decisive action to address the issue promptly. Delaying the difficult decision to terminate the employee will only exacerbate the problem, create further disruption within the team, erode morale, and potentially expose the company to further legal risks.

Terminating an employee is never an easy or pleasant decision, but it is sometimes necessary to protect the interests of the company, maintain the integrity of the legal department, and safeguard the well-being of the other team members. It is critically important to follow proper legal procedures, adhere to all applicable employment laws, and thoroughly document the specific reasons for the termination to avoid potential legal challenges, such as claims of wrongful termination, discrimination, or retaliation.

Red Flag

If other departments within the company actively avoid working with a particular member of the legal team, consistently complain about their lack of responsiveness, or express concerns about their judgment or work quality, it is a clear indication that there is a serious problem that needs to be addressed promptly. This could be due to a lack of responsiveness, poor communication skills, a general unwillingness to collaborate effectively, or a pattern of making poor decisions that have negative consequences for the business. In such cases, it is essential to conduct a thorough performance review, reassess the individual's suitability for the role, and determine whether they are the right fit for the team and the company.

Outsourcing vs. In-House: When to Bring in the Big Guns (and When to Save Money)

Not every legal issue or matter requires the specialized expertise or extensive resources of external legal counsel. Determining when to engage outside counsel and when to handle legal matters internally within the in-house legal team can result in significant cost savings, improved efficiency, and enhanced control over legal strategy for the company.

What Should Stay In-House?
- routine contracts and standard commercial agreements that are frequently used in the company's day-to-day business operations
- general employment law matters and routine HR-related legal issues, such as employee handbooks, performance management, and basic compliance with labor laws
- day-to-day regulatory compliance with industry-specific regulations and general legal requirements
- internal investigations into minor employee misconduct or policy violations (when appropriate and when there are no conflicts of interest within the legal team)

Handling these types of routine legal matters in-house allows the legal team to develop a deep and comprehensive understanding of the company's business operations, its internal policies and procedures, and its risk tolerance. This in-depth knowledge enables the legal team to provide more tailored, practical, and cost-effective legal advice that is aligned with the company's specific needs and objectives. It also allows the company to build a strong and collaborative relationship with its legal team, fostering a culture of compliance and ethical conduct throughout the organization.

Key Takeaway
Any legal work that is repetitive, relatively high-volume, and predictable should generally be handled internally by the in-house legal team to minimize expenses, maximize efficiency, and maintain control over the legal process.

When to Bring in Outside Counsel?
- high-stakes litigation that could potentially threaten the company's financial stability, its long-term viability, or its core business operations
- specialized regulatory matters that require specific expertise in niche areas of the law, such as antitrust law, data privacy and cybersecurity, international trade regulations, or complex intellectual property law
- mergers and acquisitions, including due diligence, negotiation of transaction documents, and regulatory approvals

- formal government investigations by regulatory agencies, such as
  the Securities and Exchange Commission (SEC), the Department of
  Justice (DOJ), or the Environmental Protection Agency (EPA)
- situations where impartiality and objectivity are essential, such as
  conducting highly sensitive internal investigations into allegations
  of misconduct involving senior executives or members of the board
  of directors

Engaging outside counsel in these complex and high-stakes situations provides access to specialized legal expertise, extensive resources, and in-depth experience that may not be readily available within the in-house legal team. It also ensures that the company receives objective, independent, and impartial legal advice from seasoned professionals who are experts in their respective fields.

Managing Outside Counsel Costs.
Law firms, particularly large and prestigious ones, can be very expensive, and their fees can quickly add up, potentially consuming a significant portion of the legal budget. It is essential to proactively manage outside counsel costs to ensure that the company receives good value for its investment in legal services. Here are some effective strategies for controlling outside counsel costs:

- Negotiate billing rates upfront with each law firm and clearly define the
  scope of the engagement, including the specific tasks and deliverables
  that are expected. Explore alternative fee arrangements, such as fixed
  fees for specific projects, capped fees for certain phases of litigation,
  or success-based pricing that rewards the law firm for achieving
  favorable outcomes.
- Limit unnecessary hours by ensuring that law firms are not billing for
  junior associates or paralegals performing administrative tasks that
  could be handled more efficiently and cost-effectively by internal staff.
  Also, discourage redundant research or excessive document review
  by providing clear guidance and access to relevant information.
- Assign a single internal point person within the legal team to serve
  as the primary contact for outside counsel. This will help to avoid

multiple lawyers from the law firm billing for the same updates, inquiries, or tasks, and it will streamline communication and coordination.
- Carefully audit all invoices from outside counsel to identify any discrepancies, excessive charges, or unauthorized expenses. If a law firm's bill seems unreasonable, challenge it immediately and request a detailed explanation and justification for the charges.

Proactive cost management is essential for ensuring that the company receives maximum value for its investment in outside legal services. It is important to establish clear expectations with outside counsel regarding billing practices, cost controls, and communication protocols.

Avoiding Burnout: How to Keep Your Legal Team Sane and Retained

One of the most significant and pervasive challenges faced by legal departments in today's demanding business environment is the ever-present risk of employee burnout. The constant pressure to meet deadlines, the heavy and often unpredictable workloads, the high-stakes nature of legal work, and the inherent stress levels associated with managing legal risks can take a significant toll on even the most dedicated and resilient lawyers, leading to burnout, decreased productivity, and high employee turnover. Here are some effective strategies for preventing burnout and retaining your valuable legal talent:
- Encourage delegation by empowering senior lawyers to train junior staff, mentor them in their professional development, and distribute tasks effectively to ensure that workloads are evenly balanced across the team.
- Set realistic expectations for workload and availability, avoiding the expectation of 24/7 availability, which can lead to exhaustion, resentment, and a significant decline in employee well-being.
- Invest in technology and efficiency tools, such as contract management software, document automation systems, and legal research platforms,

to automate routine legal tasks, streamline workflows, and reduce unnecessary workload on legal staff.
- Create a healthy, supportive, and inclusive work culture by recognizing and celebrating achievements, encouraging breaks and time off to recharge, promoting work-life balance, and fostering a sense of camaraderie and teamwork within the legal department.
- Offer meaningful career growth opportunities by providing talented lawyers with a clear path to advancement within the organization, offering challenging and rewarding assignments, and supporting their professional development through training, mentoring, and continuing legal education.

Burnout is a state of emotional, physical, and mental exhaustion caused by prolonged or excessive stress. It is characterized by feelings of cynicism, detachment, and a lack of accomplishment. Burnout can lead to a wide range of negative consequences, including decreased productivity, increased absenteeism, higher employee turnover, and a decline in overall employee health and well-being.

Red Flag
If your most valuable and experienced employees are consistently leaving the company, citing "better work-life balance," "lack of career growth opportunities," or "high levels of stress" as the primary reasons for their departure, it is a clear indication that your legal department has a serious burnout problem that needs to be addressed immediately. This may require a comprehensive review of workload distribution, management practices, and the overall work culture within the department.

Fostering a Culture of Continuous Learning and Development

A thriving and high-performing legal team embraces a culture of continuous learning and professional development. This not only benefits the individual lawyers by enhancing their skills, knowledge, and career prospects but also significantly enhances the overall capabilities and effectiveness of the legal department. Here are some practical and effective ways to foster a culture of continuous learning and development within your legal team:

Provide access to continuing legal education (CLE) programs, professional development courses, and industry conferences. Encourage lawyers to attend conferences, workshops, seminars, and online courses to stay up to date on the latest legal developments, regulatory changes, and emerging best practices in their respective fields.

Encourage active participation in industry associations, bar associations, and other professional organizations. These organizations provide valuable opportunities for lawyers to network with their peers, learn about best practices, contribute to the legal profession, and enhance their professional reputation.

Implement a formal mentorship program. Pair junior lawyers with experienced senior lawyers who can provide guidance, support, feedback, and career advice. This can help junior lawyers develop their legal skills, build their confidence, integrate into the team, and accelerate their professional growth.

Create opportunities for cross-training and job rotation. Allow lawyers to work on different types of legal matters, support various business units, and rotate through different areas of the legal department. This can help them develop a broader understanding of the company's operations, expand their skillset, and gain valuable experience in different areas of the law.

Support advanced education and professional certifications. Consider providing tuition reimbursement, scholarships, or other forms of financial assistance to lawyers who wish to pursue advanced degrees, professional certifications, or specialized training programs that will enhance their legal expertise and contribute to the company's success.

Leveraging Technology to Enhance Efficiency and Productivity

Technology can play a transformative role in enhancing the efficiency, productivity, and overall effectiveness of a legal team. By automating routine tasks, streamlining workflows, and providing access to powerful legal research tools, technology can free up lawyers to focus on more strategic and high-value activities. Here are some specific examples of how technology can be leveraged to improve the performance of a legal team:

Contract Management Software. Implement a comprehensive contract management system to automate the entire contract lifecycle, from initial drafting and negotiation to final execution, storage, and renewal. This can save time, reduce the risk of errors, ensure compliance with contractual obligations, and provide valuable insights into contract performance.

Document Management Systems. Utilize a robust document management system to organize and store all legal documents in a secure, centralized, and easily accessible electronic format. This can improve collaboration among team members, reduce the risk of lost or misplaced documents, and facilitate efficient retrieval of information.

Legal Research Tools. Provide lawyers with access to comprehensive legal databases, online research platforms, and artificial intelligence-powered research tools. This can help them find relevant case law, statutes, regulations, and legal precedents more quickly and efficiently, saving them valuable time and improving the accuracy of their legal analysis.

E-Discovery Software. Invest in e-discovery software to streamline the process of collecting, reviewing, and producing electronic evidence in litigation and regulatory investigations. This can save time, reduce costs, and ensure compliance with e-discovery rules.

Collaboration Tools. Utilize collaboration tools, such as shared workspaces, video conferencing platforms, and instant messaging applications, to facilitate communication and collaboration among team members, even when they are working remotely or in different locations. This can improve teamwork, reduce the risk of miscommunication, and enhance overall productivity.

AI-Powered Legal Tools. Explore the use of artificial intelligence (AI) to automate tasks such as document review, legal research, contract analysis, and compliance monitoring. AI-powered legal tools can help to improve efficiency, reduce costs, and identify potential risks and opportunities that might be missed by human lawyers.

Measuring and Evaluating Legal Team Performance

It is essential to measure and evaluate the performance of the legal team on a regular basis to ensure that it is meeting the company's needs, contributing to its overall success, and providing value for its investment. Here are some key metrics that can be used to measure legal team performance:

Cost savings. Track the amount of money that the legal team saves the company through effective negotiation, litigation avoidance, proactive risk management, and other cost-saving measures.

Risk mitigation. Measure the legal team's effectiveness in identifying, assessing, and mitigating legal risks, such as compliance violations, litigation exposure, and reputational damage.

Compliance. Track the company's compliance with applicable laws and regulations, including the number of compliance violations, the number of fines and penalties paid, and the effectiveness of compliance training programs.

Client satisfaction. Survey internal clients (i.e., other departments within the company) to assess their satisfaction with the legal services they receive from the legal team.

Employee satisfaction. Survey legal team members to assess their job satisfaction, their perceptions of the work environment, and their level of engagement. Use this feedback to identify areas for improvement and to address any concerns that employees may have.

Case outcomes. Track the outcomes of legal cases and assess the legal team's effectiveness in achieving favorable results, such as winning lawsuits, negotiating settlements, and resolving disputes.

Efficiency. Measure the legal team's efficiency in handling legal matters, such as the time it takes to complete a contract review, respond to a legal inquiry, or resolve a legal dispute.

Five-Point Framework for Building a Legal Department That Won't Burn Out

1. Core Competencies: Building a Multifaceted Legal Team

Assemble a legal team with a blend of critical skills: strategic thinking, business acumen, crisis management, excellent communication, and strong negotiation/relationship-building abilities.

- Strategic thinkers align legal advice with business goals, anticipate risks, and present actionable solutions.
- Business-savvy lawyers understand the industry, communicate in business terms, and balance innovation with risk management.
- Crisis managers prepare for and lead responses to high-stakes incidents with clear plans and cross-functional collaboration.
- Excellent communicators translate complex legal risks for non-legal audiences, ensuring clarity and buy-in.
- Negotiators and relationship builders foster trust, manage conflict, and secure mutually beneficial outcomes with internal and external stakeholders.

2. Smart Hiring and Team Development

- Hire not just for legal experience, but for judgment, cultural fit, intellectual curiosity, adaptability, communication, teamwork, empathy, ethics, initiative, attention to detail, and work ethic.
- Use scenario-based interviews to assess candidates' real-world problem-solving and alignment with company values.
- Fire decisively when necessary to protect team integrity and morale, following legal protocols and documenting reasons thoroughly.

3. Resource Allocation: In-House vs. Outsourcing
- Keep routine, high-volume, and business-integrated legal work in-house to maximize efficiency, control, and cost savings.
- Engage outside counsel for high-stakes litigation, specialized expertise, major transactions, or when independence is required.
- Proactively manage outside counsel costs through clear engagement terms, billing controls, and rigorous invoice review.

4. Preventing Burnout and Fostering Retention
- Prevent burnout by encouraging delegation, setting realistic workload expectations, leveraging technology, and promoting a supportive culture.
- Invest in career growth through mentoring, training, and clear advancement paths.
- Recognize signs of burnout and address root causes—such as workload imbalance or lack of growth opportunities—promptly.

5. Continuous Improvement and Performance Measurement
- Foster a culture of ongoing learning: support CLE, industry engagement, mentorship, and cross-training.
- Leverage technology to automate routine tasks, enhance research, and improve collaboration.
- Regularly measure legal team performance using metrics like cost savings, risk mitigation, compliance, client and employee satisfaction, case outcomes, and efficiency.
- Use feedback and data to drive improvements and ensure the legal department remains a strategic asset.

Case Studies

Scenario I: Launch of a Revolutionary AI-Powered Healthcare Platform

A dynamic *health tech* company is preparing to launch an AI-driven patient care platform aimed at transforming the delivery of healthcare services. The product integrates advanced machine learning algorithms to provide personalized treatment recommendations, streamline administrative workflows, and enhance patient engagement. However, the company faces several challenges:

- **Regulatory Complexity.** Healthcare regulations, including HIPAA, GDPR, and evolving AI-specific guidelines, present significant compliance hurdles in multiple jurisdictions.
- **Competitive Threats.** Established healthcare technology firms are rapidly developing similar AI solutions, raising concerns about intellectual property (IP) protection, data privacy, and the timing of market entry.
- **Risk Appetite.** The executive team is visionary and open to bold moves but remains cautious about potential patient safety incidents, regulatory sanctions, and reputational harm.

The company's legal team is called in to advise on the launch strategy, IP protection, and regulatory compliance.

How a Business-Savvy Lawyer Responds

1. Deep Industry and Business Understanding
The lawyer begins with a comprehensive analysis of the health tech industry, the company's AI technology, and its key performance indicators (KPIs). They review clinical validation data, study the company's risk tolerance, and monitor competitors' regulatory filings and product launches to anticipate legal and business threats.

2. Strategic Legal Advice Aligned with Business Goals
Rather than offering generic, risk-averse advice, the lawyer aligns their counsel with the company's growth ambitions and risk profile. They:

- Map out regulatory requirements for AI in healthcare across target markets, distinguishing between established rules (e.g., HIPAA in the US, GDPR in the EU) and areas of regulatory uncertainty.

- Recommend a phased rollout, prioritizing jurisdictions with clear
  digital health and AI regulations, enabling the company to gain early
  traction while monitoring regulatory developments elsewhere.
- Advise on swift IP protection for proprietary algorithms and data
  models, while suggesting business strategies such as strategic
  partnerships with healthcare providers and rapid user adoption to
  outpace competitors.

3. Clear, Business-Relevant Communication

Understanding that executives and clinicians may not be legal experts, the lawyer translates complex legal risks into actionable business language. They provide:

- A risk matrix detailing the likelihood and impact of regulatory
  intervention, patient data breaches, or AI safety incidents in
  each market.
- Financial models comparing the costs and benefits of different
  launch strategies, including potential legal exposure and lost market
  share from delays.
- Scenarios for competitor responses, such as potential IP litigation
  or regulatory complaints, and proactive mitigation strategies.

4. Proactive, Cross-Functional Collaboration

The lawyer collaborates closely with product, clinical, and compliance teams to ensure legal considerations are embedded in business planning from the outset. They:

- Lead workshops to identify operational risks, such as data privacy
  vulnerabilities or algorithmic bias, and address compliance gaps.
- Develop training materials for customer support and clinical
  staff to handle patient inquiries about data use, privacy, and
  AI-driven decisions, reducing the risk of misstatements or
  regulatory violations.

5. Balancing Innovation and Risk

Rather than hindering innovation with excessive caution or exposing the company to undue risk, the lawyer helps leadership make informed, balanced decisions. They recommend:

- Building a compliance framework that is robust yet adaptable,
  allowing the company to respond quickly as healthcare and AI
  regulations evolve.

- Establishing a crisis management plan for potential legal, safety, or reputational issues, ensuring the company can respond rapidly to patient safety incidents or regulatory investigations.

Key Takeaways

A Business-Savvy Lawyer

- Develops deep expertise in the company's industry, business model, competitive landscape, and risk tolerance to deliver guidance that supports both innovation and prudent risk management.
- Analyzes financial statements, KPIs, market trends, and profitability drivers, and communicates legal advice in clear, actionable language tailored for non-legal professionals.
- Advises on complex initiatives—such as launching an AI-powered healthcare platform—by conducting thorough industry and competitor analyses, assessing regulatory requirements, and aligning legal strategies with the company's growth ambitions.
- Maps out regulatory obligations, recommends phased market entry, secures intellectual property, and suggests business tactics to gain a competitive edge.
- Translates legal risks into business terms, provides risk matrices and financial models, and anticipates competitor and regulatory responses with proactive mitigation plans.
- Integrates legal considerations early by embedding compliance frameworks, training staff, and preparing crisis management plans to address potential legal, safety, or reputational issues.

Scenario II: Data Breach at a Mid-Sized Retailer
A mid-sized clothing retailer discovers a cybersecurity breach exposing sensitive customer data (payment details, addresses) of 500,000 users. The breach occurred due to a phishing attack on an employee, and hackers are threatening to leak the data publicly unless a ransom is paid.

How a Great Crisis Management Lawyer Responds

1. Immediate Activation of the Crisis Plan
The lawyer, pre-designated in the company's crisis management plan, swiftly coordinates with the IT, PR, and executive teams to:
> **Contain the breach.** Work with cybersecurity experts to isolate affected systems and prevent further data loss.
> **Preserve evidence.** Ensure forensic investigations adhere to legal standards for potential litigation or regulatory scrutiny.
> **Activate communication protocols.** Advise on internal and external messaging to avoid admissions of liability while maintaining transparency.

2. Legal Risk Assessment and Compliance
> **Regulatory compliance.** Confirm compliance with data breach notification laws (e.g., GDPR, CCPA), ensuring affected customers and regulators are notified within 72 hours.
> **Contractual review.** Identify obligations to third parties (e.g., payment processors, vendors) and assess liability under service agreements.
> **Litigation preparedness.** Anticipate class-action lawsuits and advise on strategies to mitigate damages, such as offering credit monitoring to affected customers.

3. Coordinated Stakeholder Management
> **Regulatory liaison.** Directly communicate with data protection authorities to demonstrate cooperation and avoid penalties.
> **Public relations.** Collaborate with PR teams to draft statements that balance legal defensibility (e.g., avoiding speculative language) with empathy for customers.
> **Employee guidance.** Address employment law concerns, such as disciplining the employee involved in the phishing incident, while ensuring compliance with labor regulations.

4. Strategic Decision-Making

Ransom negotiation. Weigh the legal and ethical implications of paying the ransom versus refusing, considering potential reputational harm and precedent-setting risks.

Insurance claims. Review cybersecurity insurance policies to expedite claims and offset financial losses.

Post-crisis review. Conduct a "lessons learned" analysis to update the crisis plan, including stronger employee training and revised data security protocols.

Key Takeaways

A Great Crisis Management Lawyer

1. Establishes Preparedness and Planning
- Develop a pre-defined, well-documented crisis management plan that assigns clear roles, responsibilities, and communication protocols for the legal team and key stakeholders.
- Gather information rapidly, assess risks, and respond strategically to minimize damage.

2. Coordinates Multi-Disciplinary Efforts
- Partner with IT, PR, and executive leadership to contain and investigate incidents.
- Preserve evidence for legal and regulatory scrutiny.
- Manage internal and external communications to balance transparency with legal protection.

3. Assesses Legal Risks and Ensures Compliance
- Ensure compliance with data breach notification laws (such as GDPR and CCPA), promptly notify affected parties and regulators, and review contractual obligations to third parties.
- Anticipate litigation and advise on mitigation strategies, such as offering credit monitoring.

4. Engages Stakeholders and Regulators
- Engage directly with regulators to demonstrate cooperation and reduce penalties.
- Collaborate with PR teams to ensure public statements are legally sound and empathetic.

• Address employment law considerations, especially regarding employees involved in the incident.

5. *Drives Strategic Decision-Making*
   • Weigh the pros and cons of actions like ransom payments, considering legal, ethical, and reputational factors.
   • Review insurance coverage and expedite claims to offset losses.

6. *Implements Continuous Improvement*
   • Conduct post-crisis reviews to update crisis management plans, improve employee training, and strengthen data security protocols.

These takeaways illustrate that great crisis management lawyers are proactive planners, decisive leaders, and strategic communicators who protect the company's interests while navigating complex legal, regulatory, and reputational challenges.

Scenario III: Contract Dispute with a Key Supplier

A multinational corporation's in-house legal team faces a contentious contract renegotiation with a long-term supplier. The supplier, facing increased costs, demands significant price hikes and less favorable delivery terms. The business unit is under pressure to maintain supply continuity and cost control, while the supplier hints at walking away if their demands are not met. The negotiation involves not only the supplier's legal counsel but also external expert witnesses on market pricing and government regulators monitoring fair trade practices. The relationship has become strained, with both sides wary of litigation but unwilling to concede easily.

How an In-House Lawyer with Strong Negotiation & Relationship-Building Skills Responds

1. Preparation and Stakeholder Mapping
- The in-house lawyer begins by thoroughly preparing, understanding the company's objectives, the business unit's needs, and the minimum acceptable terms (the "walk away" position).
- They map all stakeholders: Internal Business, Procurement, Finance, External Counsel, regulators, and the supplier's team, identifying key decision-makers and their motivations.

2. Building Rapport and Managing Tension
- Recognizing the importance of positive relationships, the lawyer initiates informal conversations with the supplier's legal counterpart, aiming to rebuild trust and open lines of communication, even engaging in small talk to humanize the process.
- They emphasize a collaborative tone, making it clear that the goal is a mutually beneficial outcome, not a zero-sum battle.

3. Active Listening and Information Gathering
- The lawyer employs active listening, asking open-ended questions to uncover the supplier's underlying interests (e.g., are the cost increases temporary or structural?).
- They gather market intelligence and consult expert witnesses to validate or challenge the supplier's claims, strengthening their negotiation position with facts.

4. Strategic Negotiation Tactics
- Using a negotiation playbook, the lawyer outlines preferred outcomes, acceptable compromises, and clear red lines, updating the playbook as talks progress.
- They remain calm and professional under pressure, using pauses and patience to avoid emotional escalation and to encourage the supplier to reveal more about their position.
- The lawyer takes rational, well-supported positions, demonstrating why proposed terms are fair and market-aligned, and invites the supplier to do the same.
- They manage expectations internally, ensuring business leaders understand both the risks of an impasse and the value of a sustainable relationship.

5. Creative Problem-Solving
- Rather than focusing solely on price, the lawyer seeks creative solutions—such as phased price adjustments, shared risk mechanisms, or longer-term commitments in exchange for concessions.
- They leverage timing and tactical flexibility, knowing when to press, when to pause, and when to escalate or de-escalate issues.

6. Maintaining Control and Professionalism
- The lawyer ensures the company retains control over the negotiation process, resisting pressure to rush or accept unfavorable terms.
- They document all agreements and insist that nothing is final until all terms are settled and signed.

7. Outcome and Relationship Management
- If a deal is reached, the lawyer ensures it is clearly documented and that both sides understand their obligations, reducing the risk of future disputes.
- If negotiations stall or the supplier's demands exceed acceptable risk, the lawyer is prepared to walk away, having already identified alternative suppliers and communicated these contingencies internally.
- Regardless of the outcome, the lawyer works to preserve a professional relationship, recognizing the potential for future dealings or industry overlap.

Key Takeaways

An In-House Lawyer with Strong Negotiation & Relationship-Building Skills

- Maps all stakeholders and prepares thoroughly by understanding company objectives, business needs, and defining clear negotiation boundaries.
- Builds rapport and manages tension by initiating informal conversations, fostering trust, and emphasizing collaboration over confrontation.
- Employs active listening and gathers critical information by asking open-ended questions, consulting expert witnesses, and validating claims with market intelligence.
- Applies strategic negotiation tactics by using a negotiation playbook, maintaining professionalism under pressure, and managing internal expectations about risks and outcomes.
- Pursues creative problem-solving by proposing flexible solutions, such as phased pricing or shared risk mechanisms, and adapting tactics as negotiations evolve.
- Maintains control and professionalism throughout the process by documenting agreements, resisting unfavorable terms, and preserving relationships for future dealings.

Final Thought: Build Smart, Not Just Fast

Creating a truly exceptional legal team is a long-term journey, not a short-term sprint. It requires strategic hiring practices, thoughtful resource allocation, a commitment to continuous improvement, and an unwavering dedication to building a sustainable and high-performing legal department. The ultimate goal is not simply to assemble a group of talented lawyers but to cultivate a well-functioning, business-savvy, and strategically aligned legal department that can effectively navigate complex legal challenges, support the company's business objectives, and protect its long-term interests, all without succumbing to the debilitating effects of stress, overwork, and burnout.

When you get this right, you will have a legal team that is not only highly effective and respected throughout the organization but also deeply committed to the company's success, personally invested in remaining a part of it for years to come, and passionate about providing outstanding legal services to help the company achieve its full potential. So, let's get to work and build a legal dream team that will propel your company to new heights of success, innovation, and ethical business practices.

SIX

FINANCIAL AND BUSINESS ACUMEN
—
MASTERING KEY METRICS

Financial and Business Acumen— Mastering Key Metrics

If you want a seat at the business table, you need to speak the language. And in corporate America, the language is finance. Not legalese. Not case law. Finance. Revenue, margins, cash flow, ROI, EPS—these are the words that move the conversation, drive decisions, and shape the strategy. If you're not fluent, you're just an observer, not a participant.

This chapter is your crash course. We're not turning you into a CFO. No one expects you to build financial models or explain deferred tax assets. But you *are* expected to understand what the CFO is worried about. You need to be able to read a financial statement and see the story it's telling. Not just the story of past performance, but the risks lurking under the surface— regulatory, contractual, operational—and how they might erupt. You need to connect the dots between what's in the 10-K and what's sitting on your legal risk register.

Because here's the hard truth: If you don't understand the company's financials, you can't spot legal risk, assess compliance exposure, or give actionable advice when it counts. You'll miss the signals. You'll offer technically correct but commercially useless guidance. And you'll get left out of the conversations that matter.

Using plain English, we'll walk through the income statement, balance sheet, and cash flow statement—not just what they are, but what they *mean* from a lawyer's perspective. We'll cover key financial metrics every GC should know cold—like EBITDA, EPS, and free cash flow—and why they matter in board meetings and SEC filings. You'll learn how to read an earnings report like a lawyer, spot red flags before the regulators do, and understand the pressure your CFO is under every quarter.

Because when you understand the numbers, you don't just give legal advice, you shape strategy. And that's what earns you the seat.

The Numbers That Matter: Understanding the Core Financial Statements

You don't need to be a CPA to be a great GC. But if you want to give real-time, real-world advice, you need to be financially fluent. You need to speak the CFO's language and spot the legal implications buried in the numbers before they explode into full-blown crises. Here's your crash course, tailored for in-house lawyers who want to be business-critical, not back-office.

Income Statement: Performance, Pressure, and Potential Pitfalls
This is the scoreboard Wall Street watches. Revenue on top. Net income—or net loss—at the bottom. But for Legal, the real action is in the middle: the assumptions, estimates, and judgment calls that shape how performance gets portrayed.

Revenue Recognition.
This is where fraud often starts and where the SEC loves to poke around. Are we recognizing revenue when the service is performed? Or are we pulling forward revenue to make the quarter? For in-house counsel, ASC 606 isn't just an accounting rule—it's a litigation trigger. Watch for:
  • multi-element arrangements (e.g., bundling services and hardware)
  • channel stuffing (pushing inventory to distributors to inflate sales)
  • side agreements with customers that change price, delivery, or return terms (often unsigned and undocumented, but very real)

These practices can give rise to misstatement risk, breach of contract claims, whistleblower complaints, and regulator interest.

Cost of Goods Sold (COGS) and Operating Expenses (OpEx).

Are costs being capitalized that should be expensed? Look at R&D, software development, or internal legal costs. Over-capitalizing expenses can inflate profits and mislead investors—classic accounting games. Pay attention to how litigation reserves are booked (or conspicuously not booked). If you've recommended an accrual and it doesn't show up, ask why. That decision might be discoverable down the road.

Non-GAAP Measures.

Adjusted EBITDA, "core" earnings, or "pro forma" results can be informative—or deceptive. What's being excluded? Stock comp? Restructuring charges? Legal settlements? Watch for recurring "non-recurring" items. You may need to review or approve earnings call scripts, investor decks, or 8-K filings where these numbers appear. If management's story diverges from GAAP results, that's a potential securities risk.

Litigation and Contingency Disclosures.

Scan the notes and MD&A (Management Discussion & Analysis) in parallel. If there's a material legal risk pending—or a loss that's probable and estimable—it should be disclosed and potentially accrued. Omitting it is a red flag. Misstating it is worse.

Watch Out For:
- sudden spikes or drops in net income without clear drivers
- unusually low legal or tax expense in a high-risk quarter
- "other income" that includes settlement proceeds, often misunderstood by investors and missed by compliance
- income smoothing—when companies make small adjustments to make earnings appear more stable

As GC, your job is to ask: Are these numbers telling the truth? And if they're not, are we ready for what happens when someone else finds out?

Balance Sheet: The Hidden Exposure Map

This is the company's financial snapshot at a single point in time—what we own, what we owe, and what the shareholders are left with. But as in-house counsel, you're reading it not just for solvency or leverage; you're looking for legal obligations, contractual landmines, and signs of aggressive risk-taking.

Assets

Accounts Receivable. A ballooning A/R balance could indicate customers aren't paying—potential contract disputes, collection risk, or even fraud (e.g., fake invoices). Check the aging schedule.

Inventory. Excess inventory might suggest poor forecasting, obsolescence, or channel stuffing. It can lead to write-downs, warranty claims, or even product liability exposure if quality control is compromised to clear stock.

Goodwill & Intangibles. These arise from acquisitions and can signal risk. If performance drops below projections, impairment charges could follow—raising questions about the diligence process, deal disclosures, and board oversight. Plaintiffs' lawyers love this.

Prepaid Expenses and Deferred Charges. Often overlooked, but sometimes where companies stash legal costs or regulatory fees to spread them over time. If the legal department is involved in a big regulatory settlement, make sure you understand the accounting treatment.

Liabilities

Accounts Payable and Accrued Liabilities. Look for spikes that may suggest unpaid obligations, vendor disputes, or delayed litigation payments.

Deferred Revenue. Often tied to contractual obligations. If the company's taken money upfront but hasn't delivered, that's not just an accounting issue; it's a customer and reputational risk.

Debt. Read the covenants. Are we close to triggering one? Are we required to disclose pending litigation? Does a material adverse event clause include regulatory investigations? You may need to coordinate with outside counsel and the treasury team on disclosures and waiver requests.

Pension & Benefit Liabilities. High exposure here can create ERISA risk, especially if underfunded plans are involved.

Equity
Stock-Based Compensation. Are option grants properly approved and disclosed? Are executive awards triggering say-on-pay or proxy advisory scrutiny?
Retained Earnings. Are dividends draining reserves that might be needed for settlements, legal judgments, or indemnification obligations?

Off-Balance-Sheet Items
This is your domain. Think:
Operating leases. Especially under ASC 842—many now back on the balance sheet.
Contingent legal liabilities and guarantees.
Indemnification agreements and earn-outs from M&A deals.
Joint venture or partnership risks. Where you have legal exposure without formal control.

If it's "off book," that doesn't mean it's off your radar.

Cash Flow Statement: The Canary in the Coal Mine

If the income statement tells a story and the balance sheet shows your resources, the cash flow statement reveals what's real. It shows where the money is coming from and where it's going—and whether the company can afford to do what it's legally or contractually obligated to do.

Operating Activities.

Start here. This is the cash the business generates from its core operations. It should align (at least directionally) with net income. If not, something's off. Look at:
Working Capital Changes. If receivables and inventory are rising faster than sales, that's a red flag. If payables are stretching out, the company might be preserving cash in a way that breaches supplier terms.

Accrual Reversals. If litigation accruals suddenly disappear or drop with no real change in risk, dig in. That might be a quiet push to boost earnings—or a sign the legal team isn't being heard.

Deferred Revenue Movements. Sharp drops might signal contract cancellations, refunds, or legal disputes over performance.

Investing Activities.

This includes capital expenditures (CapEx), M&A, and divestitures. For Legal:

CapEx. Big infrastructure or tech investments often require contracts, regulatory reviews, and compliance oversight. You should know where the money is going.

Acquisitions. These are legal minefields. Diligence, reps and warranties, integration risks—all are your problem. If the company is spending heavily on deals, make sure you're looped in early.

Asset Sales. These may mask earnings issues. What's being sold? At what price? To whom? Are there liabilities being transferred or retained? Are there buyer indemnities you'll need to enforce later?

Financing Activities.

This includes issuing debt or equity, repaying loans, paying dividends, or buying back stock. Each carries legal implications:

Debt Raises. Review offering documents and regulatory filings. Know what's being promised to lenders or investors.

Stock Buybacks. Ensure compliance with safe harbors and insider trading policies. Timing around earnings releases can raise red flags.

Dividends. If cash is tight, dividend declarations can raise fiduciary duty concerns—especially in states with "surplus" requirements for lawful dividends.

Free Cash Flow (FCF).

This isn't GAAP, but it's gospel to investors. It measures what's left after CapEx and operating expenses. If FCF is weak, the company may not be able to fund litigation, settlements, or regulatory compliance without new financing. That means legal risk = financial risk.

Numbers tell a story, but not always the whole story. As in-house counsel, your job is to read between the lines. To understand when financial performance is being managed too tightly, when accounting choices become legal issues, and when the company's financial picture exposes it to legal, regulatory, or reputational blowback.

Because at the end of the day, legal risk doesn't just come from lawsuits—it comes from how the company presents itself to the world. And those presentations almost always start—and sometimes end—with the financial statements.

Key Metrics You Must Know: And Why

Earnings Per Share (EPS)

EPS isn't just a performance metric. It's the battleground for investor confidence, executive compensation, and—when things go sideways—plaintiff's exhibits. When EPS misses forecasts, activist investors get louder, boards get restless, and litigation risk goes up. A GC must ask, "How much of EPS is driven by real operational performance versus financial engineering like stock buybacks?" If EPS is climbing while revenue is flat or declining, that's a red flag. Are one-time charges being excluded to inflate "adjusted" EPS? What's the company telling the market—and more importantly, is it telling the truth? Misleading disclosures about EPS can trigger securities litigation, SEC scrutiny, or reputational blowback. You don't have to calculate it, but you do have to question it.

EBITDA (Earnings Before Interest, Taxes, Depreciation, and Amortization)

EBITDA is often marketed as a "pure" view of operating performance, free from the messiness of capital structure, tax strategy, or non-cash expenses. But it's also a playground for creative accounting. "Adjusted EBITDA" can be gamed to remove anything inconvenient—restructuring costs, litigation reserves, even stock-based compensation. As GC, you need to know how it's calculated and what's being excluded. Why? Because EBITDA often underpins debt covenants, drives acquisition valuations, and influences executive bonuses. If a covenant breaches due to manipulated EBITDA figures, you're on the hook to manage the fallout—regulatory, contractual, or reputational.

Free Cash Flow (FCF)

FCF is what's left after the company pays the bills and reinvests in the business. It's the money that funds dividends, stock buybacks, acquisitions, and legal settlements. If FCF is strong, you have flexibility. If it's weak, you're operating on a financial tightrope. You may find yourself deferring a settlement, slow walking a compliance program, or prioritizing one litigation matter over another because the company literally can't afford to do more. GCs must track FCF trends and understand what drives them, such as CapEx spikes, inventory build-ups, and payment delays. Legal strategy isn't just about risk; it's about affordability.

Gross Margin

This measures how efficiently a company turns revenue into profit after accounting for the cost of goods sold. A shrinking gross margin could mean rising input costs, pricing pressure, or operational inefficiencies, all of which can invite investor scrutiny and erode shareholder value. For GCs, a falling margin might foreshadow upcoming cost-cutting measures (think headcount reductions or facility closures), which come with legal implications—from WARN Act compliance to labor litigation. It also matters in contract negotiations: margins affect the tolerance for risk allocation and indemnities.

Operating Margin

Operating margin digs deeper than gross margin, factoring in the full spectrum of operating expenses—R&D, SG&A, and more. For in-house counsel, this is a proxy for how lean—or bloated—the company's cost structure really is. A narrowing operating margin might prompt aggressive cost containment, and that usually comes with legal friction: terminations, vendor disputes, and slashed compliance budgets. It also speaks volumes about management's discipline, which should influence how you approach risk, governance, and long-term legal planning.

Return on Invested Capital (ROIC)

ROIC measures how well a company turns capital into profit. It's the litmus test for whether growth creates value. If ROIC is lower than the company's cost of capital, the business is destroying value, even if revenue is growing. For GCs, a low ROIC should prompt caution around M&A, expansion plans, and long-term commitments. It also invites shareholder activism—especially if the company is sitting on cash or chasing deals that look like empire-building. If you're not asking the hard questions about capital allocation, someone else will.

Total Shareholder Return (TSR)

TSR combines stock price appreciation with dividends. It's the scorecard investors really care about. And it's increasingly tied to executive compensation, proxy fights, and director retention. A lagging TSR can bring activist pressure, class actions, and PR headaches. For the legal department, this means more time defending decisions made by leadership—sometimes in court, often in the court of public opinion. GCs must understand what's driving TSR—market conditions, peer performance, or internal missteps—and prepare for the legal consequences if performance sags.

Debt-to-Equity Ratio

This ratio shows how much the company relies on borrowed money. A highly leveraged company has less flexibility, higher interest obligations, and greater bankruptcy risk. For in-house lawyers, that affects everything from negotiating credit agreements to assessing the company's ability to absorb litigation losses or regulatory fines. If the balance sheet is stretched, even minor legal problems can become existential. Don't assume the CFO has this under control. Know the leverage, ask the hard questions, and factor it into your risk assessments.

Working Capital

This is the company's short-term liquidity—the difference between current assets and current liabilities. When working capital is tight, everything slows down: vendor payments, contract execution, even legal billing. It's a leading indicator of financial stress. If the company is squeezing vendors or delaying payments, disputes and lawsuits follow. If receivables are ballooning, your customers might be facing cash flow issues, which become your problem when they default. Legal risk often shows up in the cracks of working capital management. Watch for them.

Key Takeaway

These aren't just finance metrics. They're legal early warning systems. They shape the company's strategic choices, affect your legal budget, and determine how much risk the business can tolerate. If you're not paying attention, you're flying blind. And if you want a real seat at the table, fluency in these numbers isn't optional; it's mandatory.

Inside the CFO's Head: What Keeps Them Up at Night

A CFO's world is about balancing short-term performance with long-term sustainability, all under intense scrutiny. Here's what's rattling around in their head (and why Legal should care):

Revenue Recognition

Are we recognizing revenue in compliance with ASC 606? Have we clearly identified performance obligations, and are we meeting them before booking the revenue? Is someone pulling forward revenue to hit a quarterly target? Are we walking the line—or crossing it—with channel stuffing or premature shipments? Revenue recognition issues are a compliance minefield. They don't just trigger restatements; they can trigger subpoenas. If the CFO is nervous, you should be too. Revenue problems are where accounting questions turn into SEC investigations and securities fraud lawsuits.

Cash Flow Management

CFOs live and die by working capital. Is cash coming in fast enough to cover payroll, capital projects, and debt service? Are we stretching payables or factoring receivables to make the numbers look better than they are?

Are we close to breaching debt covenants that could trigger default or force renegotiations? When liquidity gets tight, Legal gets looped in—fast. Desperate companies may delay disclosing bad news, get creative with accounting, or make risky bets. If cash is constrained, Legal should be asking: Where is the company exposed? What are we not being told?

Forecast Accuracy

The Street doesn't like surprises. Miss a quarter, and your stock gets punished. Miss two, and the board gets jumpy. Miss three, and the plaintiffs' bar starts circling. CFOs are under relentless pressure to deliver consistent, predictable results. But reality doesn't always cooperate. Are forecasts being sanded down to keep guidance believable, or inflated to buy time? Is the business underperforming, and are there risks we're not disclosing? Legal should be actively involved in reviewing earnings guidance and risk disclosures—not just rubber-stamping them. If the numbers don't look right, speak up.

Margin Compression

Are rising input costs eating into gross margins? Are we in a pricing war we can't win? Are cost cuts threatening long-term growth or increasing operational risk? Margin compression is one of the clearest signals of trouble ahead. When margins shrink, CFOs scramble to fix it—sometimes by cutting corners, pushing questionable deals, or deferring necessary investments. Legal should be attuned to whether margin pressures are distorting decision-making or incentivizing behavior that could cross ethical or legal lines.

> **Debt and Capital Structure.** Are we over-leveraged? Do we have the flexibility to raise capital if needed? Are we violating any debt covenants? Is our credit rating in jeopardy? CFOs constantly monitor the company's financial stability. Refinancing risks, interest rate exposure, and investor confidence are all part of the capital structure calculus. Legal must be on top of what's in the credit agreements, what triggers defaults, and what the risks are in a downturn. A poorly timed downgrade or breach can create a full-blown crisis.

M&A and Strategic Initiatives. Are we buying the right target, or buying trouble? Are we divesting a core asset and underplaying the long-term impact? Are we disclosing enough about the risks of a deal? CFOs are deeply involved in strategic transactions, but the legal implications are just as critical. Overpaying, *under-diligencing*, or under-disclosing in a material transaction can haunt the company for years. GCs should be side-by-side with the CFO in every deal room— scrutinizing assumptions, challenging rosy projections, and flagging hidden liabilities.

Tax Risk and Regulatory Exposure. Are we pushing too hard on tax optimization strategies? Are we exposed to regulatory shifts—domestic or international—that could materially affect our business? Tax and regulatory risk may not make headlines until they explode, but CFOs obsess over them. Aggressive tax positions, global transfer pricing issues, or unreported liabilities can all turn into audit nightmares or enforcement actions. Legal should ensure that Finance isn't playing games with tax interpretations or ignoring red flags.

Cybersecurity and Operational Disruption. What happens if we get hacked? What's our exposure if key systems go down or operations are disrupted? Cyber risk is no longer just an IT concern; it's a financial and legal risk with real bottom-line implications. CFOs are increasingly accountable for understanding the cost of a breach, the adequacy of insurance, and the potential impact on earnings. GCs should be working with CFOs and CISOs to ensure disclosures are accurate, response plans are sound, and that no one is minimizing risk to preserve appearances.

ESG and Reputational Risk. Are we *walking the walk* on sustainability, DEI, and governance, or just spinning a good story? CFOs are realizing that ESG matters not just to regulators and activists, but to investors, customers, and employees. If the company overpromises and underdelivers, it's not just bad optics; it's securities fraud waiting to happen. Legal should be part of the ESG reporting process, reviewing statements for accuracy, and ensuring the company's walk matches its talk.

Key Takeaway
You don't need to manage the balance sheet, but you do need to understand what's on it, how it's being presented, and what keeps your CFO sweating at 3 a.m. Because where the CFO sees numbers, you should see risk.

How Financial Decisions Drive Legal Risk

Business decisions don't happen in a vacuum; they carry legal consequences. Finance may be setting the course, but Legal is responsible for helping the company steer clear of the rocks. Here's how financial strategy can quietly load the company with legal landmines:

Cost Cutting
Cutting costs is rarely just about spreadsheets. Layoffs can trigger federal and state WARN Act requirements, especially if they cross numerical thresholds. Get it wrong, and you're facing statutory damages, back pay, and class action risk. Selective terminations can give rise to discrimination or retaliation claims, especially if the reductions are not clearly documented or are perceived as targeting protected classes. Cutting compliance or audit functions to "save money" might score short-term gains, but it's an engraved invitation for regulatory investigations, particularly in industries where scrutiny is high. Think healthcare, financial services, and government contracting.

M&A Activity
Deals move fast, and sometimes they move stupid. Legal is often looped in to paper the transaction, but the smarter move is to challenge the deal's assumptions early. Are the financial forecasts built on shaky ground? That's a recipe for securities fraud claims post-closing. Are the representations and warranties truly backed by clean diligence, or are you buying a portfolio of ticking time bombs—unresolved litigation, regulatory noncompliance, or weak IP protection? If shareholders think the company overpaid (or undersold), expect breach of fiduciary duty claims, especially in public company contexts where disclosure and fairness are paramount.

Capital Allocation

Share buybacks can look great on a PowerPoint slide, but if done around earnings announcements or while executives are trading stock, they raise insider trading and market manipulation concerns. "Was this buyback program used to hit EPS targets that drove bonus payouts?" If so, plaintiffs' firms and the SEC are watching. Similarly, if dividends are sustained while the company is bleeding cash, you may hear from creditors—or worse, a bankruptcy judge—about fraudulent conveyance or breach of fiduciary duty to creditors.

Debt Issuance

Every loan has strings attached. Miss a covenant, and you don't just default; you may trip cross-defaults in other instruments or violate material adverse change clauses that open the door to litigation. Complex financing often includes negative covenants that constrain operational flexibility: acquisitions, capex, and even hiring. If business units act outside those guardrails, you're not just non-compliant; you may be in breach. The GC needs a seat at the table during term sheet negotiations, not just when the loan agreement shows up for signature.

Revenue Recognition Strategies

Sales targets create pressure. That pressure can lead to channel stuffing, bill-and-hold arrangements, or premature revenue recognition that may technically boost top-line results, but violate ASC 606 or GAAP, resulting in restatements, SEC investigations, or shareholder derivative suits. Legal should help Finance draw the line between aggressive and illegal.

Tax Optimization Tactics

Everyone wants to "optimize the effective tax rate," but if it involves shifting profits to low-tax jurisdictions without actual substance (people, risk, capital), the company could be facing transfer pricing disputes, BEPS (Base Erosion and Profit Shifting) enforcement, or reputational damage when the tax structure hits the front page of the Wall Street Journal. The line between smart tax planning and aggressive evasion is thinner than it looks—and Legal needs to help draw it.

Executive Compensation Design

Tie bonuses to the wrong financial metrics—especially adjusted ones—and you may be incentivizing behavior that increases compliance risk. Are "non-GAAP" earnings being used to justify payouts that don't reflect real performance? Boards have faced SEC scrutiny and shareholder litigation for approving comp plans that misalign incentives or reward short-term manipulation over long-term health.

Liquidity Management and Vendor Stretching

CFOs under cash pressure often stretch payables—delaying vendor payments to preserve liquidity. But if the company appears solvent while it's essentially insolvent, those delays could be viewed as preferential payments in bankruptcy or fraudulent conveyances. Add in contract breaches and vendor litigation, and the short-term "solution" starts to look legally expensive.

Asset Sales and Restructurings

Disposing of underperforming business units can make financial sense, but if done too fast or too opaquely, they can attract fraudulent transfer claims, antitrust scrutiny, or contractual liability if counterparties claim their rights were ignored. If pension liabilities or environmental obligations are involved, the risks multiply.

Stock-Based Acquisitions and Dilution

Acquisitions paid for in equity can lead to dilution litigation, particularly if insiders are perceived to benefit disproportionately or if the company fails to adequately disclose dilution impacts to existing shareholders. Public company GCs should assume that every material issuance is being reviewed for fairness, disclosure accuracy, and process integrity.

Key Takeaway

When Finance pulls a lever, Legal must know what's connected to the other end. Every financial decision creates a web of legal exposure—contractual, regulatory, fiduciary, reputational. The biggest legal problems often come dressed as financial strategy. Your job is to see them coming before anyone else does.

Reading an Earnings Report Like a Business Advisor Instead of Like a Lawyer

Earnings calls and 10-Qs aren't bedtime reading. They're where risk and opportunity hide in plain sight.

Overly Optimistic Language
Look for hype masquerading as analysis. Words like *"unprecedented demand,"* *"industry-leading margins,"* and *"game-changing technology"* are great for marketing—but if they're not backed by credible data or grounded in measurable outcomes, they're a lawsuit waiting to happen. Puffery may be legally defensible in some cases, but it erodes trust and invites scrutiny—especially from plaintiffs' lawyers, short-sellers, and regulators.

Footnotes
This is where the real story lives. Don't just skim. Dig into the footnotes for subtle shifts: increased reserves for pending litigation, new investigations, or changes in the way revenue is recognized. Did the company suddenly reverse a valuation allowance? That might suggest they're banking on future tax gains to make earnings look better. Footnotes are the CFO's confession booth—quiet, technical, but telling.

GAAP vs. Non-GAAP Metrics
Non-GAAP is where fantasy accounting thrives. Adjusted EBITDA, pro forma net income, and other "custom" measures can paint a prettier picture, but you must ask: *What's being excluded, and why?* If they're stripping out stock-based compensation, restructuring charges, or ongoing legal expenses as if they're one-offs, be suspicious. If the company always "adjusts" its way to a beat, the legal department should be asking hard questions.

MD&A Analysis (Management's Discussion & Analysis)

This section should bridge what happened and what's next. Does it explain the actual business drivers behind the numbers? Or does it dance around bad quarters with jargon and euphemisms? Vague MD&A is a red flag. So is silence on known headwinds—regulatory pressure, supply chain issues, or contract disputes. Remember: the SEC expects companies to disclose *material known trends and uncertainties.* If they aren't doing that, the legal department is complicit in the risk.

Segment Results

Revenue and margin trends in the segment breakdown can tell you where the business is truly strong—or bleeding cash. Are high-growth claims concentrated in a tiny sliver of the business? Are "international" operations propping up domestic stagnation? Segments often reveal contradictions in the rosy headlines. Legal needs to be on alert for segments under investigation, subject to sanctions, or exposed to geopolitical risk.

Quarterly Guidance and Revisions

How confident is management about the future? Are they reaffirming guidance, raising it, or walking it back? When companies miss and then say, "We're confident about the back half of the year," that optimism needs to be stress-tested. Legal should evaluate whether guidance reflects actual data or wishful thinking—and if there's a pattern of overpromising and underdelivering, that's a disclosure risk.

Legal Proceedings Section

This often gets boilerplate treatment, but it shouldn't. Is a major new lawsuit downplayed as "routine"? Are there material settlements that aren't quantified? Has a known regulatory investigation gone from civil to criminal without any change in the disclosure? Push for specificity; vague language may avoid panic today, but it can set up securities fraud claims tomorrow.

Cash Flow Statement: Money In, Money Out

It's not just for accountants. Look at cash from operations versus net income. Is the company "earning" money on paper but burning cash in reality? Are they financing growth with debt or issuing equity? If free cash flow is negative but the company is increasing dividends or buying back stock, it's time to question priorities—and whether shareholders are being misled.

The Proxy Statement: Where Governance Meets Risk

A proxy report is closely linked to the earnings report, and they often reference each other. Lawyers often treat the proxy like a compliance checklist. But if you read it like a business advisor, you'll see it's a roadmap to the company's real priorities and a preview of where legal risk may erupt.

What In-House Counsel Should Focus on in the Proxy

Executive Compensation and Pay-for-Performance Alignment. How is management *incentivized*? If the CEO gets bonuses for EBITDA growth, are they cutting corners on safety, compliance, or ethics to hit the numbers? If stock options are heavily used, is there a risk of backdating or manipulation? Compensation structures drive behavior. Misaligned incentives aren't just governance risks—they're litigation traps.

Risk Oversight Disclosures. Who owns risk at the board level? Is the full board responsible, or is it delegated to the audit or risk committee? Are emerging risks—like cybersecurity, AI, climate, and human capital— specifically mentioned? If the company claims strong oversight but the disclosures are thin, it could come back to bite them when a crisis hits.

Board Composition and Expertise. Does the board have the right mix of industry experience, financial literacy, and independence? Are there red flags, such as overly boarded directors, lack of diversity, or tenure imbalances? A weak or unengaged board is a governance risk, and plaintiffs will argue it enabled mismanagement or failed in its fiduciary duties.

Shareholder Proposals and Voting Trends. What are investors worried about? Climate disclosure? Political spending? DEI commitments? Pay equity? Even if the board recommends a "no" vote, large support levels for shareholder proposals are signals that should shape legal risk strategy. Ignoring them doesn't make the pressure go away; it just postpones the reckoning.

Related Party Transactions. Is the company doing business with insiders, directors, or their affiliates? These can be legal and aboveboard, but they're also hot spots for conflicts of interest and reputational risk. Look for patterns or increasing volume year-over-year. One shady transaction can tank a deal or trigger a derivative suit.

Audit Committee Report. How robust is the audit committee's oversight? Do they meet frequently? Are they engaging independent advisors? A thin audit committee disclosure may indicate box-checking rather than real diligence. And if there's aggressive revenue recognition or questionable internal controls, the committee will be Exhibit A in any future litigation.

CEO Pay Ratio. It's not just optics. If the CEO-to-median employee pay ratio is astronomical, it can inflame unions, employees, activists, and the press. In litigation, it can also undermine claims of cost discipline or fairness in restructuring. It's a cultural lightning rod, and GCs need to be ready to defend it.

Clawback and Hedging Policies. Do they exist? Are they enforced? Weak or missing clawback provisions send a message that bad behavior won't be punished. And if execs are allowed to hedge their equity awards, that undermines the alignment with shareholder interests the comp plan claims to promote.

Key Takeaway

Don't just read earnings reports and proxy statements. Interrogate them. They're not just investor documents; they're legal risk disclosures in disguise. If you want to be seen as a business partner, you need to read between the lines, challenge assumptions, and connect the dots before the market—or a plaintiff's lawyer—does.

Five-Point Framework for Demonstrating Financial and Business Acumen

1. Speak the CFO's Language: Financial Fluency Is Non-Negotiable

What It Means
If you want a seat at the strategy table, you need to speak finance fluently. That includes understanding the **income statement, balance sheet, and cash flow statement**—and reading between the lines.

GC Priorities
- Know how revenue is recognized (ASC 606), what drives EBITDA, and what's buried in non-GAAP metrics.
- Analyze working capital movements, covenant compliance, and debt service capacity.
- Translate financial performance into legal exposure: Are reserves being understated? Is revenue recognition aggressive? Is CapEx masking operational risk?

Why It Matters
If you don't understand what the numbers are hiding, you can't see the legal landmines buried underneath them. Finance is the language of strategy; learn to speak it, or risk becoming irrelevant.

2. Align Legal Oversight with Financial Strategy

What It Means
Every financial lever—buybacks, M&A, debt issuance, cost cutting—carries legal risk. You must be upstream, not downstream, in financial decision-making.

GC Priorities
Capital Allocation. Know whether buybacks or dividends are being used to inflate EPS or mask weak free cash flow.
M&A. Evaluate not just diligence, but assumptions underpinning deal value and integration risk.

Cost Cuts. Evaluate WARN Act exposure, discrimination risks, and long-term compliance erosion.

Debt and Liquidity. Understand covenant structures, default triggers, and how litigation may affect solvency.

Why It Matters.

Most legal crises begin as a financial strategy. The GC must be a guardrail, not a mop.

3. Read Earnings Reports Like a Prosecutor, Not a PR Rep

What It Means

Earnings calls, 10-Qs, and proxy statements aren't marketing material; they're legal exhibits in the making. Treat them accordingly.

GC Priorities
- Scrutinize MD&A and footnotes for buried risks: restatements, reversals, regulatory exposure.
- Challenge "adjusted" metrics that exclude recurring legal, stock comp, or restructuring costs.
- Assess forward-looking statements and guidance language for puffery or omission liability.
- Ensure proxy disclosures align compensation with performance—and clawbacks with accountability.

Why It Matters

Misleading disclosure doesn't just kill trust—it draws subpoenas. Your job is to prevent tomorrow's litigation today.

4. Understand the CFO's Pressure Points: and Stay Ahead of Them

What It Means

To be indispensable, you need to know what's keeping the CFO awake at night—and anticipate the legal fallout before it happens.

GC Priorities
- Track margin compression, forecast fragility, and liquidity stress signals.
- Understand how operational disruptions (e.g., cybersecurity breaches or vendor defaults) can balloon into disclosure issues or fiduciary crises.
- Engage on ESG, DEI, and reputational risk—not just compliance, but perception.

Why It Matters
If the CFO is sweating, the GC should be sounding the alarm. Your job is to see around corners before the market (or the board) demands answers.

5. Use Metrics as Early Warning Systems, Not Just Scorecards

What It Means
Key financial metrics are more than performance indicators—they are early alerts for legal exposure, governance gaps, and strategy blind spots.

GC Priorities
EPS. Is it real growth or financial engineering? Legal must scrutinize what's driving the number.

Free Cash Flow. If it's weak, can the company afford compliance, settlements, or headcount?

ROIC and TSR. Poor returns and lagging shareholder value invite activism and fiduciary claims.

Debt-to-equity and working capital. Legal risk increases as financial flexibility shrinks.

Why It Matters
Legal risk often shows up first in the numbers—if you know where to look. Track the right metrics, and you'll spot problems before they become headlines.

Case Studies

Scenario I: The CFO's Sleepless Night, and the GC Who Saw it Coming

It's the end of Q3 at Apex Tech, a publicly traded software company. The CFO, Lisa Chen, has just reviewed the preliminary financials. They look . . . fine. Maybe too fine. Revenue is up. EPS meets guidance. But something feels off. Lisa can't sleep.

What's Keeping Her Up

Revenue Recognition

Sales jumped 18% . . . on paper. But a closer look shows a surge in end-of-quarter transactions with unusually generous payment terms and unclear implementation timelines. The sales team insists it's legit. But Lisa worries these "sales" might not meet the performance obligation requirements under ASC 606.

Cash Flow Management

DSO (days sales outstanding) has ballooned from 42 to 67 days. AR is growing faster than revenue. Meanwhile, vendors are quietly complaining about delayed payments. There's just enough cash in the system to get by, but Lisa knows they're skating on thin ice.

Forecast Accuracy

Next quarter's guidance assumes a major enterprise renewal goes through. But Legal is still negotiating the indemnity clauses, and there's chatter that the client might walk. If the deal doesn't land, guidance is toast—and so is their credibility with analysts.

Debt Covenants

A new $150M revolving credit facility has a debt-to-EBITDA covenant that's about to get tight. If they miss projections or adjust EBITDA too aggressively, they could be in violation.

Compression

Cloud hosting costs have surged, eating into gross margins. Product is pushing price cuts to close deals, but ops hasn't cut costs to match. The result: margins are slipping, and the board is noticing.

Enter: The General Counsel, Maria Ramos

Maria had seen the red flags building. Earlier in the quarter, she raised questions about:

Aggressive revenue recognition. She flagged vague contract terms and pressured Finance to consult outside auditors.

Forecast assumptions. She asked whether key deals were truly committed or still up in the air.

Adjusted EBITDA games. She challenged why they were backing out legal reserves and restructuring costs from the "adjusted" metric used in investor calls.

Debt covenants. She sat down with Lisa and reminded her that misjudging compliance risk, however technical, could trigger disclosure obligations.

When Maria reviewed the draft 10-Q, she didn't just do a legal scrub; she asked hard questions about what wasn't being said.

The Result

Lisa brought Maria into the CFO-CEO pre-earnings huddle.
Together, they:

Pushed back on premature revenue recognition. Some deals were reclassified as deferred revenue.

Softened forward-looking audience and added more risk disclosure around large renewals.

Updated the MD&A section to reflect liquidity pressures and covenant sensitivity.

Resisted the urge to over-polish the EBITDA story and instead offered a transparent reconciliation.

The Street didn't love the earnings call. But they respected it. No lawsuits. No restatement. No crisis.

Key Takeaway

The CFO may be the one lying awake at night, but a sharp GC keeps them from waking up to subpoenas. When Legal understands what's inside the CFO's head, they don't just protect the company. They earn their seat at the strategy table.

Scenario II: The CFO's Bold Move—and the Legal Blowback

Tech Nova Inc., a mid-cap public SaaS company, was under pressure. Revenue growth had slowed, the stock was lagging the market, and a hedge fund had taken a 6% stake and was getting noisy. The CFO, eager to show the Street that the company could still deliver value, rolled out a multi-pronged financial strategy:

1. Cut $50M in costs, primarily through layoffs and downsizing internal audit.
2. Launch a $200M share buyback program.
3. Announce a $300M acquisition of a smaller AI firm—paid for entirely in stock.
4. Delay vendor payments by an additional 45 days to conserve cash.

What Went Wrong, and Why Legal Wasn't Looping in Soon Enough

Cost Cutting

HR implemented layoffs quickly, but the WARN Act threshold was miscalculated in one state. Dozens of employees received no notice. To make matters worse, two recently laid-off engineers filed EEOC complaints, claiming the layoffs disproportionately impacted employees over 50. Internal audit, now understaffed, missed early signs of revenue recognition issues in one of TechNova's foreign subsidiaries.

Buybacks and Insider Trading Allegations

The buyback launched just days before Q1 earnings were announced. Unbeknownst to the legal team, several executives had recently sold shares through 10b5-1 plans. Plaintiffs' firms pounced, alleging the company manipulated EPS and insiders timed their trades based on non-public buyback plans. A class action lawsuit followed.

The AI Acquisition

The deal press release trumpeted "transformational synergies," but the diligence was shallow. Legal hadn't vetted the target's IP—two of its core patents were subject to ongoing litigation. Worse, the AI firm's two founders had previously been subject to an SEC investigation for revenue misstatements at another company. Now, shareholders are filing derivative suits, claiming breach of fiduciary duty for failing to vet the deal or disclose known risks.

Vendor Stretching and Contract Breaches
The 45-day extension on payables sounded smart until a key cloud services vendor cut off access due to nonpayment, impacting customer-facing systems. The vendor sued for breach of contract and reputational harm. Customers noticed. Tech Nova's churn rate spiked, and so did inbound claims.

Stock-Based Acquisition and Dilution
The all-stock acquisition diluted existing shareholders by 10%, but that impact wasn't clearly spelled out in the investor presentation. One activist shareholder accused the board of using the deal to entrench management and enrich insiders. A second-class action alleged misleading disclosures and sought to enjoin the transaction.

The Result
Tech Nova's stock dropped 18% in two weeks. Analysts downgraded the company. The board demanded answers. Legal, once seen as back-office, was now front and center, playing defense.

Key Takeaway
Finance made the moves. Legal didn't ask the right questions early enough. Each financial decision created a chain of legal consequences, some of which could've been prevented with early legal engagement, better cross-functional alignment, and a sharper eye for downstream risk.

This scenario illustrates what happens when Legal is reactive instead of proactive. The message to GCs is clear: **get upstream**. If you're not involved when financial strategies are crafted, you'll be stuck cleaning up the mess after it explodes.

Scenario III: The Illusion of Performance—and the Lawsuit That Followed

MedAxis Therapeutics is a mid-cap biotech firm with a pipeline of promising but unproven therapies. In its latest earnings release, MedAxis reported record "adjusted EBITDA" and issued a glowing press release touting *"transformational revenue growth"* and *"strong momentum heading into the second half."* The stock popped 12% after the earnings call. On the surface, things looked great.

But the GC wasn't convinced, and here's why.

Red Flags the Legal Team Spotted

Footnotes buried in the 10-Q revealed a $35 million increase in legal reserves for a DOJ investigation tied to off-label marketing practices. This was downplayed on the call as "a routine matter."

- The **non-GAAP EBITDA** excluded recurring litigation expenses, stock-based compensation, and a "one-time" supply chain disruption—for the fourth quarter in a row.
- The **MD&A** was silent on a looming CMS reimbursement rule change that could gut revenue from its main drug.
- The **proxy statement** showed the CEO's bonus was heavily weighted toward hitting EBITDA targets—and that no clawback policy was in place. Meanwhile, a shareholder proposal requesting a clawback policy had received 43% support the year prior and was ignored by the board.

What the GC Did

Instead of rubber-stamping the disclosure package, the GC:

- flagged the overly aggressive tone of the earnings release and asked for toned-down language that reflected regulatory risk.
- pushed the CFO and CEO to explain the justification for excluding recurring costs in the non-GAAP metrics. When the reasoning didn't hold water, the GC insisted on revised language that more clearly outlined the risks.
- alerted the board's audit committee to the discrepancy between executive incentives and emerging litigation exposure.
- recommended revisiting the shareholder proposal on clawbacks, considering the ongoing DOJ matter.

What Happened Next

The company softened its guidance and revised its MD&A to include the reimbursement risk. The updated proxy for the annual meeting included a proposed clawback policy and more robust disclosure about the board's risk oversight process. The board also reduced the CEO's short-term incentive award to reflect unresolved legal issues.

Six months later, after the DOJ formally charged MedAxis with civil False Claims Act violations, the company's stock took a hit, but avoided a full-scale investor revolt. No securities class action was filed. Why? Because the disclosures—while not rosy—were now candid and complete.

Key Takeaways

The GC's business-savvy approach turned a potential disaster into a survivable event. By treating the earnings report and proxy statement not as check-the-box filings but as strategic documents, the GC helped the company:

- get ahead of litigation and reputational risk
- rein in management overreach
- rebuild investor trust
- strengthen governance before the lawsuits came calling

Because sometimes the best legal defense is a good set of footnotes—and a GC who *reads* them.

This isn't about turning GCs into accountants. It's about **turning them into strategic leaders**. When you read financials like a litigator, understand incentives like a board member, and translate risk like a CFO, you're not just protecting the company. You're shaping its future.

SEVEN

SEC, EARNINGS CALLS, AND DISCLOSURE LANDMINES
–
WALKING THE REGULATORY TIGHTROPE

SEC, Earnings Calls, and Disclosure Landmines—Walking the Regulatory Tightrope

As the General Counsel of a public company, you've inherited one of the trickiest legal balancing acts in corporate America. One wrong statement on an earnings call, one overly optimistic forecast in an investor presentation, or one delayed 8-K filing, and suddenly you're on the receiving end of an SEC inquiry, a shareholder lawsuit, or a headline you never wanted to see.

Disclosure rules aren't just bureaucratic red tape; they are the regulatory framework that keeps the markets fair (or at least as fair as they can be). And as GC, you are the last line of defense between your company and a financial or legal disaster. Your job is to ensure that every piece of information released to the public is accurate, timely, and compliant with SEC regulations. Fail to do so, and the consequences can range from stock drops to multimillion-dollar penalties.

No pressure, right?

Let's get you up to speed on what you must know to protect your company—and yourself.

Historical Context

The imperative for rigorous SEC regulations stems from a series of historical market failures and corporate scandals. The aftermath of the Great Depression led to the creation of the SEC in 1934, with a mandate to restore investor confidence by mandating transparency and preventing fraud. Landmark legislation like the Securities Act of 1933 and the Securities Exchange Act of 1934 laid the groundwork for modern disclosure requirements. Subsequent scandals, such as Enron and WorldCom in the early 2000s, triggered the Sarbanes-Oxley Act (SOX) of 2002, which strengthened internal controls and increased accountability for corporate executives. The 2008 financial crisis further underscored the need for robust regulatory oversight and led to the Dodd-Frank Wall Street Reform and Consumer Protection Act of 2010, which enhanced whistleblower protections and expanded SEC enforcement powers. These historical events serve as stark reminders of the potential consequences of inadequate disclosure and the critical role of the GC in upholding ethical and legal standards. Recent events such as the collapses of FTX and Celsius, and the related investigations by the SEC, have emphasized the need for transparent and accurate disclosures in the cryptocurrency space.

The GC's Role as Gatekeeper

The General Counsel is more than just a legal advisor; they are a strategic partner to the CEO and board of directors, providing counsel on a wide range of issues, from securities law compliance to corporate governance best practices. The GC's responsibilities extend beyond simply reacting to legal challenges; they also include proactively identifying and mitigating potential risks. This requires establishing robust internal controls, implementing comprehensive training programs for employees, and fostering a corporate culture that prioritizes transparency and ethical conduct. A key aspect of this role is fostering open communication within the organization, ensuring that all relevant departments understand their responsibility in the disclosure process.

Consequences of Non-Compliance

The consequences of failing to comply with SEC regulations can be severe and far-reaching. In addition to financial penalties, which can range from hundreds of thousands to millions of dollars, companies may also face reputational damage, which can be even more costly in the long run. A damaged reputation can lead to a loss of customer trust, difficulty attracting and retaining employees, and a decline in shareholder value. In some cases, executives may also face criminal charges, particularly if they are found to have intentionally misled investors.

The Public Company Disclosure Framework: What You Need to Know

When it comes to corporate disclosure, the SEC has four primary mandates: transparency, accuracy, completeness, and timeliness. Every public company is required to provide investors with clear and complete financial and operational information. The key regulatory filings that govern public company disclosures are the 10-K, 10-Q, 8-K, and the Proxy Statement—your new best friends (or worst nightmares, depending on the circumstances).

SEC Mandates

Transparency. Public companies must provide clear and understandable information about their financial performance, business operations, and risk factors. This means avoiding technical jargon and presenting information in a way that is accessible to the average investor. The SEC's plain English rules are a key component of this mandate, requiring companies to use clear and concise language in their disclosures.

> **Legal Definition.** Transparency requires disclosing information in a clear, unambiguous, and readily accessible manner, ensuring that investors can easily understand the company's financial condition and prospects.

Example. A company must clearly explain its revenue recognition policies in the 10-K, avoiding complex accounting terminology and providing illustrative examples. Using charts and graphs to visually represent financial data can also enhance transparency.

Accuracy. All information disclosed to the public must be accurate and reliable. This means ensuring that financial statements are prepared in accordance with Generally Accepted Accounting Principles (GAAP) and that all material information is verified by qualified professionals. The audit committee plays a crucial role in ensuring the accuracy of financial reporting.

Legal Definition. Accuracy demands that all disclosed information is free from material misstatements or omissions, reflecting a true and fair view of the company's financial position.

Example. If a company discovers an error in its previously issued financial statements, it must promptly correct the error and disclose the corrected information to investors. This often requires restating the financial statements, which can be a costly and time-consuming process.

Completeness. Companies must disclose all material information that investors need to make informed decisions. This includes not only positive information but also negative information that could affect the company's financial performance or prospects. The definition of "materiality" is subjective and depends on the specific facts and circumstances.

Legal Definition. Completeness necessitates the disclosure of all information that a reasonable investor would consider important in making an investment decision, including both positive and negative aspects.

Example. A company that is facing a significant legal challenge must disclose the potential impact of the litigation on its financial statements. This disclosure should include an estimate of the potential loss or range of loss, if possible.

Timeliness. Information must be disclosed to the public in a timely manner. This means filing reports with the SEC by the required deadlines and promptly disclosing any material events that could affect the company's stock price. The SEC has strict deadlines for filing the 10-K, 10-Q, and 8-K, and companies must adhere to these deadlines to avoid penalties.

> **Legal Definition.** Timeliness requires the prompt disclosure of material information, ensuring that investors have access to up-to-date information when making investment decisions.

> **Example.** A company that experiences a data breach that could affect its customers must promptly disclose the breach to investors and regulators. This disclosure should include the nature of the breach, the number of customers affected, and the steps the company is taking to mitigate the damage.

Disclosure Requirements for Foreign Companies

Foreign companies listed on U.S. exchanges are subject to the same disclosure requirements as domestic companies, with some exceptions. For example, foreign companies may be permitted to file financial statements prepared in accordance with International Financial Reporting Standards (IFRS) rather than GAAP. However, they must still provide a reconciliation to GAAP. Additionally, foreign companies may be required to disclose information about their home country's regulatory environment and any risks associated with operating in that country. The SEC has also increased its scrutiny of Chinese companies listed on U.S. exchanges, requiring them to provide greater transparency about their ownership structure and financial relationships.

The Role of Technology

Technology is rapidly transforming the landscape of corporate disclosure. Companies are increasingly using AI and data analytics to improve the accuracy and efficiency of their reporting processes. For example, AI can be used to identify potential errors in financial statements and to automate the process of preparing SEC filings. However, technology also presents new challenges for corporate disclosure. Companies must ensure that their data is secure and that their systems are not vulnerable to cyberattacks. They must also be mindful of the potential for bias in AI algorithms and take steps to mitigate this risk. XBRL (eXtensible Business Reporting Language) is increasingly important, as it standardizes financial reporting data, making it easier for investors and analysts to compare companies. The SEC mandates the use of XBRL for most filings to enhance data analysis and accessibility. Blockchain technology is also emerging as a potential tool for improving the transparency and security of corporate disclosures.

The Big Four: 10-K, 10-Q, 8-K, and the Proxy Statement

1. The 10-K: The Full Financial Picture

Think of the 10-K as your company's annual report card. This comprehensive filing contains audited financial statements, management's discussion and analysis (MD&A), risk factors, and details about business operations. It's where investors, analysts, and regulators go to get the complete picture of a company's financial health.

MD&A

The Management's Discussion and Analysis (MD&A) section is a critical component of the 10-K. It provides management's perspective on the company's financial performance, including explanations of significant changes in financial condition and results of operations. The MD&A should be a clear and concise narrative that helps investors understand the key drivers of the company's performance and the challenges it faces. The SEC has issued guidance on the MD&A, emphasizing the need for forward-looking information and a focus on key performance indicators.

Risk Factors

Disclosing relevant and up-to-date risk factors is crucial for informing investors about the potential challenges and uncertainties that the company faces. These risk factors should be specific to the company and its industry, avoiding generic boilerplate language. The SEC has emphasized the need for company-specific and tailored risk factor disclosures. It is important to regularly review and update the risk factors to reflect changes in the company's business and the external environment.

Internal Controls Over Financial Reporting (ICFR)
Section 404 of the Sarbanes-Oxley Act (SOX) requires public companies to establish and maintain internal controls over financial reporting. This includes designing and implementing policies and procedures to ensure that financial statements are prepared accurately and reliably. The company's management must assess the effectiveness of its ICFR and disclose any material weaknesses in its 10-K. The external auditor must also attest to the effectiveness of the company's ICFR. The Public Company Accounting Oversight Board (PCAOB) oversees the audits of public companies and has issued guidance on ICFR.

Internal Controls Over Financial Reporting (ICFR)
Section 404 of the Sarbanes-Oxley Act (SOX) requires public companies to establish and maintain internal controls over financial reporting. This includes designing and implementing policies and procedures to ensure that financial statements are prepared accurately and reliably. The company's management must assess the effectiveness of its ICFR and disclose any material weaknesses in its 10-K. The external auditor must also attest to the effectiveness of the company's ICFR. The Public Company Accounting Oversight Board (PCAOB) oversees the audits of public companies and has issued guidance on ICFR.

Practical Tips for Preparation
Preparing a high-quality 10-K requires effective collaboration between Legal, Finance, and other departments. Here are some practical tips:
- Start the preparation process early.
- Establish a clear timeline and assign responsibilities.
- Involve all relevant stakeholders.
- Review the 10-K carefully for accuracy and completeness.
- Obtain sign-off from senior management and the board of directors.

- Ensure consistency between the 10-K and other public disclosures.
- Utilize technology to streamline the preparation process.
- Consider conducting a "dry run" of the 10-K to identify any potential issues before filing.

2. The 10: Quarterly Check-Ups

If the 10-K is the full medical exam, the 10-Q is the quarterly check-up. Filed three times a year, these reports provide unaudited financial statements and a snapshot of recent performance.

Consistency Issues (In-Depth)

If your company suddenly changes its revenue recognition policies without explanation, expect questions from investors and regulators. Maintaining consistent accounting policies from quarter to quarter is crucial for ensuring comparability of financial information. Any changes in accounting policies must be clearly explained in the 10-Q, along with the reasons for the change and the impact on the financial statements. The SEC requires companies to disclose any material changes in accounting policies in the 10-Q.

Liquidity Concerns

If cash flow is tight, you need to disclose risks and strategies before investors read about it elsewhere. Disclosing information about the company's liquidity is essential for helping investors assess its ability to meet its short-term obligations. Key metrics to monitor include working capital, cash flow from operations, and the current ratio. Companies should also disclose any potential risks to their liquidity, such as a decline in sales or an increase in expenses.

Key Metrics. Companies should monitor and disclose trends related to cash conversion cycle, accounts receivable turnover, and inventory turnover. These metrics can provide valuable insights into the company's liquidity and efficiency.

Material Events

Any significant events between quarterly filings must be addressed (see 8-Ks below). The 10-Q must disclose any material events that have occurred since the last annual report, such as significant acquisitions, divestitures, or changes in management. The definition of "materiality" is subjective and depends on the specific facts and circumstances.

Legal Considerations
The 10-Q is subject to the same legal standards as the 10-K, including Section 10(b) of the Securities Exchange Act of 1934 and Rule 10b-5, which prohibit false or misleading statements in connection with the purchase or sale of securities. Companies should carefully review their 10-Q filings to ensure that they are accurate, complete, and not misleading.

Comparative Analysis
The 10-Q should include a comparative analysis of the company's current performance with previous quarters and the corresponding quarter of the prior year. This analysis should explain any significant variances and the reasons for the variances. The SEC has emphasized the need for meaningful comparative analysis in the 10-Q.

3. The 8-K: The 'Oh, By the Way' Filing

The 8-K is how public companies report major events—executive departures, mergers, lawsuits, bankruptcies, earnings guidance changes, or any other material event that investors need to know about within four business days.

Triggering Events (Comprehensive List)
The SEC mandates the filing of an 8-K for a wide range of events, including but not limited to:

Item 1.01: Entry into a Material Definitive Agreement. This includes contracts, leases, and other agreements that are significant to the company's business.

Item 1.02: Termination of a Material Definitive Agreement. Disclosure is required when a significant agreement is terminated, potentially impacting the company's operations or financial condition.

Item 2.01: Completion of Acquisition or Disposition of Assets. Major asset transactions must be disclosed to inform investors of changes in the company's holdings.

Item 2.02: Results of Operations and Financial Condition. This is used to announce earnings releases, providing key financial data and management's analysis. Regulation FD considerations are paramount here.

Item 2.03: Creation of a Direct Financial Obligation or an Obligation under an Off-Balance Sheet Arrangement of a Registrant. New debt or other financial obligations must be disclosed.

Item 2.04: Triggering Events That Accelerate or Increase a Direct Financial Obligation or an Obligation under an Off-Balance Sheet Arrangement. Any events that trigger acceleration or an increase in financial obligations require disclosure.

Item 2.05: Costs Associated with Exit or Disposal Activities. If a company incurs significant costs related to exiting a business segment or disposing of assets, this must be reported.

Item 2.06: Material Impairments. Any material impairments to the company's assets require disclosure.

Item 3.01: Notice of Delisting or Failure to Satisfy a Continued Listing Rule or Standard; Transfer of Listing. If the company receives notice of delisting from an exchange, this must be promptly disclosed.

Item 3.02: Unregistered Sales of Equity Securities. Any sales of equity securities that are not registered with the SEC must be reported.

Item 3.03: Material Modifications to Rights of Security Holders. Any material changes to the rights of security holders must be disclosed.

Item 4.01: Changes in Registrant's Certifying Accountant. If the company changes its auditor, this must be disclosed, along with the reasons for the change.

Item 4.02: Non-Reliance on Previously Issued Financial Statements or a Related Audit Report or Completed Interim Review. If the company determines that its previously issued financial statements should no longer be relied upon, this must be disclosed. This often requires a restatement of the financial statements, which can have significant implications for the company.

Item 5.01: Changes in Control of Registrant. A change in control of the company requires immediate disclosure.

Item 5.02: Departure of Directors or Certain Officers, Election of Directors, Appointment of Certain Officers, and Compensatory Arrangements of Certain Officers. This covers changes in the company's leadership team. The disclosure should include the reasons for the departure, election, or appointment, as well as any compensatory arrangements.

Item 5.03: Amendments to Articles of Incorporation or Bylaws; Change in Fiscal Year. Any amendments to the company's governing documents or a change in its fiscal year must be disclosed.

Item 5.05: Material Nonpublic Information. Selective disclosure of material nonpublic information (MNPI) can trigger Reg FD violations; thus, any release of MNPI must be accompanied by an 8-K filing.

Item 7.01: Regulation FD Disclosure. As mentioned above, this is the catch-all for Regulation FD compliance.

Item 8.01: Other Events. This can be used to disclose any other material events that are not covered by the other items. This item should be used sparingly and only for events that are truly material to investors.

The 8-K Trap

Failure to File. Late filings raise red flags with regulators and investors alike.

Downplaying Negative News. If the company is facing a crisis, vague language or omission of critical facts can worsen legal exposure.

Overhyping Positive News. Overstating a deal's impact or revenue potential could lead to shareholder litigation when expectations aren't met.

Best Practices for Filing

- Establish a cross-functional team responsible for identifying and evaluating potential 8-K triggering events.
- Develop a detailed checklist of events that require disclosure.
- Implement a system for tracking deadlines and ensuring timely filings.
- Review all 8-K filings carefully for accuracy and completeness.
- Consult with legal counsel to ensure compliance with SEC regulations.
- Maintain a record of all 8-K filings and supporting documentation.
- Develop a crisis communication plan to address potential 8-K triggering events.

The Four-Day Deadline

The SEC requires companies to file 8-Ks within four business days of the triggering event. This short timeframe can put significant pressure on companies, especially when dealing with complex or sensitive issues. It is crucial to have well-defined procedures in place to ensure compliance with this deadline. Companies should have a system in place for quickly gathering and verifying information related to potential 8-K triggering events.

Relationship to Other Filings

Information disclosed in an 8-K should be consistent with information disclosed in other filings, such as the 10-K and 10-Q. If there are any inconsistencies, they should be explained clearly in the filings. Companies should review their other filings to ensure they are consistent with the information disclosed in the 8-K.

4. The Proxy Statement: Governance, Executive Pay, and Shareholder Rights

The Proxy Statement (Form DEF 14A) is often overlooked but is a crucial disclosure document. It provides details on board composition, executive compensation, shareholder proposals, and corporate governance policies. Investors and activist shareholders scrutinize it closely to assess management decisions and governance effectiveness. The SEC has issued guidance on the proxy statement, emphasizing the need for clear and transparent disclosure of executive compensation and corporate governance practices.

Executive Compensation Disclosures

Pay-for-Performance Metrics. Pay-for-performance metrics must be clearly explained, or expect shareholder backlash. The proxy statement should include a detailed discussion of the company's compensation policies and how they align with company performance.

Board Independence Issues. Ensure that director independence is well-documented and properly disclosed. The proxy statement should include a discussion of the company's standards for determining director independence and any relationships that could potentially compromise a director's independence.

Key Risks

Executive Compensation Disclosures. Pay-for-performance metrics must be clearly explained or expect shareholder backlash.

Board Independence Issues. Ensure that director independence is well-documented and properly disclosed. The proxy statement should include a discussion of the company's standards for determining director independence and any relationships that could potentially compromise a director's independence.

Shareholder Proposals. Any omission of significant shareholder concerns can trigger lawsuits or regulatory interventions. The proxy statement should include a discussion of any shareholder proposals that have been submitted to the company, as well as the company's recommendations on how shareholders should vote on the proposals.

Lack of Transparency. If the proxy statement is difficult to understand or lacks transparency, investors may lose confidence in the company's management and governance practices.

Inaccurate Information. If the proxy statement contains inaccurate or misleading information, the company could face legal action from shareholders or the SEC.

Responding to Activist Campaigns. Companies should have a plan in place for responding to activist campaigns. This plan should include strategies for engaging with activists, defending against their proposals, and communicating with shareholders.

Best Practices for Preparing the Proxy Statement

- Start the preparation process early.
- Establish a clear timeline and assign responsibilities.
- Involve all relevant stakeholders.
- Review the proxy statement carefully for accuracy and completeness.
- Obtain sign-off from senior management and the board of directors.
- Ensure consistency between the proxy statement and other public disclosures.
- Utilize technology to streamline the preparation process.
- Consider engaging a proxy solicitor to assist with the preparation and distribution of the proxy statement.

Additional Considerations

ESG Disclosures. Companies are increasingly being asked to disclose information about their environmental, social, and governance (ESG) practices. This information is often included in the proxy statement.

Cybersecurity Disclosures. Companies should disclose information about their cybersecurity risks and policies in the proxy statement.

Earnings Calls: The Tightrope Walk Between Transparency and Liability

Earnings calls are where things get particularly dangerous. These quarterly conference calls with analysts and investors are designed to provide insights into financial performance, but one off-the-cuff remark from an executive can send the stock price into freefall or trigger regulatory scrutiny.

As GC, your role is to script the tightrope walk, ensuring the company is transparent without creating unnecessary legal exposure.

Best Practices

Prepare a Detailed Script. Develop a detailed script for the earnings call, including key financial metrics, management's analysis of the results, and forward-looking statements.

Practice and rehearse. Practice and rehearse the script with the executives who will be participating in the earnings call.

Monitor the Q&A Session. Monitor the Q&A session in real-time and be prepared to intervene if an executive strays too far or discloses MNPI.

Review the Transcript. Review the transcript of the earnings call to identify any potential issues.

Consult with Legal Counsel. Consult with legal counsel to ensure that the earnings call is compliant with all applicable laws and regulations.

The Three Golden Rules of Earnings Calls

1. **Stick to the Script.** Earnings calls should follow a carefully prepared script—no improvisation. Every number, statement, and forward-looking

comment should be vetted in advance. CEO and CFO enthusiasm is great, but unchecked optimism can lead to lawsuits if projections don't materialize.

Best Practices for Script Preparation
- Involve Legal, Finance, and Investor Relations in the preparation of the script.
- Ensure that the script is accurate, complete, and not misleading.
- Include a discussion of the company's key performance indicators (KPIs).
- Provide a clear and concise explanation of the company's financial results.
- Include a discussion of the company's prospects.
- Include the required safe harbor disclaimer for forward-looking statements.

2. No Off-the-Cuff Guidance. One of the biggest mistakes executives make on earnings calls is implying guidance changes without formally updating SEC filings. A careless statement like, "We're on track to exceed expectations this quarter," can be interpreted as material nonpublic information (MNPI) if it diverges from prior guidance.

Examples of Statements That Could Be Interpreted as MNPI
- "We're seeing stronger-than-expected demand for our products."
- "We expect to beat consensus estimates for the quarter."
- "We're on track to achieve our long-term growth targets."

GC Action Plan
- Train executives to deflect speculative questions (e.g., "We aren't providing additional guidance at this time.")
- Ensure all forward-looking statements include the required safe harbor disclaimer.

3. Take Care with Q&A Sessions. While the scripted portion of the earnings call can be controlled, the Q&A session is where things get risky. Analysts are trained to extract valuable tidbits of non-public information, and executives often fall into the trap of giving just a little more context.

GC's Role
- Monitor in real time—be prepared to intervene if an executive strays too far.
- Ensure Regulation FD compliance (Fair Disclosure rule)—no selective disclosure of material information.
- Conduct post-call reviews to identify and mitigate any potential issues.

Regulation FD Compliance

Regulation FD (Fair Disclosure) prohibits companies from selectively disclosing material nonpublic information to analysts or investors without simultaneously disclosing the information to the public. This rule is designed to prevent insider trading and to ensure that all investors have access to the same information at the same time.

Best Practices for Regulation FD Compliance
- Avoid selectively disclosing MNPI to analysts or investors.
- If you inadvertently disclose MNPI, immediately disclose the information to the public.
- Designate a spokesperson to communicate with analysts and investors.
- Train employees on Regulation FD and the importance of avoiding the selective disclosure of MNPI.

Common Disclosure Landmines That Can Get You in Trouble
Even experienced GCs can run into problems if they aren't vigilant. Here are some of the most common disclosure landmines that lead to SEC investigations and shareholder lawsuits:

1. Overly Optimistic Forward-Looking Statements.
Projecting unrealistic growth or success rates can lead to liability, especially if not accompanied by appropriate disclaimers and a reasonable basis.
> **Example.** A solar energy company, fueled by initial success, projects massive expansion and profitability in its 10-K without disclosing significant challenges in scaling its technology and increasing

competition. When these challenges materialize, and the company fails to meet projections, shareholders sue, alleging the 10-K was misleading. **Preventive Measures.** Base projections on solid data and documented assumptions, disclose known risks, and avoid using unqualified language like "guaranteed" or "certain."

2. Failure to Disclose Related-Party Transactions.

Any transaction between the company and its executives, directors, or major shareholders must be fully disclosed.

Example. The CEO secretly leases a property he owns to the company without board approval or proper disclosure. The SEC investigates when the arrangement becomes public, alleging a conflict of interest and failure to provide transparent information to shareholders.
Preventive Measures. Implement a robust related-party transaction policy, require annual disclosures from executives and directors, and ensure independent review and approval by the audit committee.

3. Inadequate Disclosure of Cybersecurity Risks.

In today's digital landscape, failing to disclose known vulnerabilities or past data breaches is a major oversight.

Example. A retail company experiences a significant data breach but downplays the incident in its 8-K filing, stating it had "minimal impact." When the full scope of the breach is revealed, including millions of customers' personal data compromised, shareholders file suit, alleging inadequate disclosure and misleading statements.
Preventive Measures. Conduct regular risk assessments, disclose known vulnerabilities, and provide timely and accurate information about any data breaches.

4. Misleading Non-GAAP Financial Measures.

Using metrics that aren't based on Generally Accepted Accounting Principles (GAAP) can be tricky.

Example. A tech firm heavily promotes "Adjusted EBITDA" in its earnings releases while excluding significant operating expenses, presenting a rosier picture than GAAP results would show. The SEC questions the omission, alleging that the non-GAAP measure was used to mislead investors.

Preventive Measures. Ensure non-GAAP measures are clearly defined, reconciled to the most directly comparable GAAP measure, and not given undue prominence over GAAP results.

5. Downplaying Environmental Liabilities.
Companies must disclose potential environmental liabilities, such as cleanup costs or regulatory fines.

Example. A manufacturing company fails to disclose known soil contamination at one of its plants.

Preventive Measures. Conduct regular environmental audits and assessments to identify potential liabilities and provide detailed disclosures about these risks.

6. Inadequate Discussion of Supply Chain Risks.
Supply chain disruptions can have a significant impact on a company's financial performance, and these risks must be disclosed.

Example. A clothing retailer fails to disclose its reliance on overseas manufacturing and fails to properly account for political instability.

Preventive Measures. Create contingency plans to deal with supply chain disruptions.

Five-Point Framework for Disclosure Risk Management

1. The Four Pillars of SEC Disclosure: TACT
Every disclosure must meet the SEC's gold standard:
- Transparency—Clear, plain-English explanations with charts or visuals were helpful.
- Accuracy—No material misstatements or omissions; errors must be promptly corrected.
- Completeness—Include both good and bad news; "materiality" is judged in hindsight.

- Timeliness—Disclose material events *immediately*, not after a strategy session.

GC Actions
- Embed TACT into every 10-K, 10-Q, 8-K, and earnings script.
- Use pre-mortem scenarios to anticipate what *could* be seen as incomplete or misleading.
- Make TACT the lens through which you review every sentence that touches the public.

2. Disclosure Governance: Build and Enforce the Infrastructure

Disclosure isn't a legal memo—it's a cross-functional team sport. Governance is what keeps it from becoming chaos.

GC Responsibilities
- Create and lead a **Disclosure Committee** (Legal, Finance, IR, Compliance, and IT).
- Implement **pre-clearance protocols** for all external comms (press releases, investor decks, analyst meetings).
- Maintain and enforce **checklists for 8-K trigger events**, Reg FD compliance, and proxy drafting.
- Use **technology** (XBRL, AI tools, version control systems) to manage processes and prevent mismatches.

3. Control the Narrative: Master the Earnings Call Lifecycle

Earnings calls are high-wire acts—where one off-script remark can trigger an SEC investigation or class action.

GC Must-Do's
> **Script it, rehearse it, review it.** No improvisation. Every stat should match filed disclosures.
> **Q&A Planning.** Pre-script answers to sensitive areas. Train execs on "bridge" language.
> **Live Monitoring.** Have Legal and IR on deck during the call to intervene or deflect.

Post-Call Scrub. Review transcript, identify MNPI risks, and prepare for comment letters or follow-ups.

Remember: Earnings calls are one step away from being deposition transcripts.

4. Stay Ahead of the Landmines

The most dangerous mistakes are the ones that seem minor—until they're not. A great GC sees them coming.

Landmines to Watch For
- overly optimistic forward-looking statements without disclaimers or data support
- undisclosed related-party transactions
- misleading or overly prominent non-GAAP financial metrics
- vague or incomplete cyber risk disclosures
- downplayed environmental, regulatory, or supply chain risks

Mitigation Toolkit
- Require legal review of *all* investor-facing materials.
- Regularly update internal training on Reg FD, MNPI, and cyber disclosure.
- Centralize disclosure oversight—no more "someone else was handling it."

5. Culture and Courage: Elevate Compliance to the C-Suite

The most effective GCs don't just manage disclosures—they shape the culture that makes them accurate in the first place.

Leadership Principles
- Frame disclosure as a **trust-building exercise**, not just a compliance box.
- Speak truth to power—escalate red flags, even when it's uncomfortable.
- Empower your team to spot issues early, not just fix them late.
- Model transparency yourself—GCs are held to higher standards in crises.

A great GC doesn't just *file* disclosures. They *own* the entire ecosystem that makes those filings accurate, timely, and credible. That means embedding this 5-point framework into the culture of the company—so that by the time the 10-K is due, the hardest work is already done.

———————————

Case Studies

Scenario I: AI, XBRL, and the Unexpected Disclosure Crisis at NovaLytix Corp.

NovaLytix Corp., a fast-growing cloud-based analytics company listed on NASDAQ, prided itself on being ahead of the curve when it came to financial disclosure technology. The company had recently implemented a sophisticated AI-powered system to prepare its 10-Q filings, designed to flag anomalies and automate the drafting of key sections. It also used XBRL tagging to meet SEC requirements and ensure investors had quick access to standardized, machine-readable data.

Everything ran smoothly—until it didn't.

Two days before the filing deadline for Q2, the AI system flagged a potential discrepancy in revenue recognition tied to a new long-term contract with a large healthcare client. The system suggested the revenue had been prematurely recognized under ASC 606. The finance team, under pressure, manually overrode the flag without escalating it to the audit committee, trusting the system's initial configuration and assuming it was a false positive.

Unbeknownst to them, the override created a new issue. The XBRL tags used to categorize the revised revenue data weren't updated. As a result, the numbers in the text of the 10-Q didn't match the tagged data, an inconsistency that was immediately picked up by investors using XBRL-compliant analysis tools.

Within hours of the filing going live, a well-known analyst publicly questioned the integrity of NovaLytix's revenue reporting on social media. The company's stock dropped 8% in a day. The SEC sent a routine comment letter that quickly escalated into an informal inquiry.

To make matters worse, a follow-up internal audit revealed that the AI system's machine-learning model had been trained on biased historical data, leading it to under-flag revenue issues for deals with long-term payment schedules—particularly common in the company's healthcare sector business. And while NovaLytix's blockchain-based financial archive helped validate the authenticity and timestamp of prior filings, it did nothing to prevent the actual misclassification error.

Key Takeaways

> **AI is a tool, not a replacement for judgment.** The finance team's blind trust in automation—and lack of escalation—undermined the system's utility.

Bias in algorithms is real. Training data must be scrutinized to ensure AI doesn't replicate or amplify systemic reporting weaknesses.

XBRL tagging errors are not harmless. Investors rely on this standardized data, and inconsistencies can erode credibility fast.

Technology can create transparency or confusion. It all depends on how well it's governed.

Cyber risk isn't the only threat. Even without a hack, disclosure failures stemming from system misconfigurations can lead to reputational and regulatory crises.

NovaLytix ultimately restated its financials, revamped its internal controls around AI use in financial reporting, and established a disclosure committee with oversight of technology-integrated reporting tools.

Scenario II: Preparing the 10-K at Solventa BioTech

Solventa BioTech, a mid-sized publicly traded pharmaceutical company, was preparing its annual 10-K. The prior year's filing had been rushed, resulting in inconsistencies between the 10-K and earnings press releases, triggering a comment letter from the SEC and an uncomfortable call with the audit committee. Determined to avoid a repeat, the General Counsel, CFO, and Chief Accounting Officer took a new approach.

Here's how the process played out

Starting Early. In early October—three months before the year-end—Solventa kicked off a cross-functional planning session. Legal, Finance, Investor Relations, HR, Internal Audit, and Compliance all had seats at the table.

Clear Timeline & Accountability. The team created a detailed project plan using project management software. Each section of the 10-K—from MD&A to risk factors to executive compensation—was assigned a lead, with deadlines mapped to the filing date.

Stakeholder Involvement. The legal team reviewed litigation contingencies and disclosure trends; IR helped ensure alignment with investor messaging; HR coordinated the CD&A section; and IT ensured the XBRL tagging would be ready on time.

"Dry Run" Review. In mid-December, the team conducted a full draft walkthrough, flagging redundancies, confusing language, and gaps—like a new product launch mentioned in the earnings call but missing from the MD&A. They caught it before the SEC or investors did.

Consistency & Sign-off. The final draft was reviewed by senior management and shared with the board's audit committee. The GC cross-checked all public statements for consistency. The CFO and CEO signed off with confidence.

Technology Enablement. Using disclosure management software, version control was automated and collaborative editing streamlined, avoiding last-minute email confusion and formatting disasters.

Result

A clean 10-K filing, no SEC comments, and praise from the board. More importantly, the process strengthened cross-departmental trust and reduced future risk—demonstrating the power of proactive, coordinated disclosure.

Scenario III: The Crosswind Communications Misstep

Crosswind Communications, a mid-cap telecom company, had a turbulent Q3. On October 3rd, it finalized a $150 million acquisition of a regional broadband provider—triggering Item 2.01 (Acquisition of Assets). On the same day, its CFO abruptly resigned due to "personal reasons," implicating Item 5.02 (Officer Departure). Just days later, the company's auditors flagged a potential material weakness in its internal controls related to revenue recognition, raising Item 4.02 (Non-Reliance on Financials) concerns.

Instead of filing timely 8-Ks, Crosswind tried to contain the news. Leadership issued a vague press release about "executive transitions" and "continued growth," without filing a corresponding 8-K or disclosing the audit issues. Meanwhile, investor relations hinted at "significant synergies" from the acquisition during private calls with analysts, without making the same information public, violating Regulation FD.

Two weeks later, after media reports surfaced and the stock began to drop, Crosswind scrambled to file a consolidated 8-K—late, incomplete, and full of corporate spin. The SEC launched an inquiry into disclosure practices. A class-action lawsuit followed, alleging securities fraud and material omissions.

Key Takeaways

Crosswind's failure to promptly and transparently file required 8-Ks magnified its legal risk and eroded investor trust. The 8-K isn't optional; it's a legal obligation and a critical tool for credibility. Companies must treat it not as an afterthought, but as an immediate, accurate, and plain-English communication of material developments.

Scenario IV: The Resignation That Almost Sparked an SEC Inquiry

On a quiet Tuesday morning, the CFO of Orion Biologics, a mid-cap biotech firm, submitted her unexpected resignation, citing "personal reasons." The news quickly sent ripples through the executive suite—but the real trouble started when no one could agree on whether this triggered an 8-K filing.

The legal team assumed HR would notify them of any filing obligations. HR thought Finance had it covered. And Finance was still trying to understand whether this qualified as a "material event" under Item 5.02 of the 8-K. By Thursday morning—three business days later—a junior IR analyst flagged the resignation as a potential 8-K issue based on a checklist she found in an old training binder. Panic ensued.

The company scrambled. The GC convened an emergency meeting with Legal, HR, Finance, and Corporate Communications. They confirmed the resignation *was* material—especially given that the CFO had been scheduled to present at a major investor conference the following week. Now, they had less than 24 hours to file.

They rushed to draft the 8-K but ran into a new issue: the draft stated that the resignation "was not expected," while the upcoming 10-Q—already in near-final form—referenced "planned transitions in leadership." The inconsistency raised red flags.

Fortunately, Orion had recently implemented a crisis protocol requiring Legal to cross-check disclosures across all filings. The GC caught the inconsistency, updated the language in the 10-Q, and worked with IR to prepare a short statement for analysts. The 8-K was filed late Friday afternoon—within the four-day window, but barely.

Key Takeaways

Cross-functional coordination is essential—every function assumed someone else was handling it.

Checklists and training saved the day: an outdated binder still proved more useful than institutional memory.

Deadline pressure is real—the four-day rule is not generous, especially for sensitive events.

Consistency across filings avoids regulatory scrutiny and investor confusion.

Crisis communication plans help stabilize the message externally when material events arise unexpectedly.

Had Orion not already begun building better disclosure processes, the situation could have escalated quickly into an SEC comment letter or worse.

Scenario V: The Slippery Slope on Q3 Earnings Call—A Case Study in Preventing Legal Exposure

BrightWave Technologies Inc., a mid-cap public SaaS company, is preparing for its Q3 earnings call. The company has experienced a mixed quarter: revenues are slightly below consensus, but bookings for next quarter are strong, and customer churn has dropped significantly. The CFO, known for his enthusiastic delivery, is eager to frame the numbers as a sign of accelerating momentum. The General Counsel, Marissa Chen, is a former SEC enforcement attorney who knows how dangerous an optimistic throwaway line can be.

Pre-Call Preparation

Marissa assembles the cross-functional disclosure team—Finance, Legal, IR, and the CEO/CFO—for a two-week preparation sprint.

Script Development. The script is drafted with input from Finance (for numbers and KPIs), IR (for investor messaging), and Legal (for disclosure risk). Every data point is tied back to public filings. Any reference to next quarter's expectations is couched in conditional language and paired with the required safe harbor statement.

Anticipating Q&A Landmines. Marissa compiles a list of likely analyst questions—especially around the new AI product's adoption rate and margin expansion. She red-flags any speculative projections and coaches the CEO and CFO on how to bridge confidently without straying into guidance.

Dry Run. A full rehearsal is held two days before the call.

During the mock Q&A, the CFO slips and says, "I think we'll see a revenue bounce next quarter as the AI pipeline converts."

Marissa cuts in immediately, "Let's remember that any outlook has to align with filed guidance. We'll revisit that phrasing to make sure it's Regulation FD compliant."

That line is struck from their talking points.

The Earnings Call

Scripted Remarks. The CEO and CFO stick to the script. Financials are explained clearly, challenges are acknowledged (slower international sales), and opportunities are framed cautiously. All forward-looking statements are properly qualified.

Q&A Session. The Real-Time Tightrope: An analyst asks, "Can you tell us whether AI product revenues will outpace legacy software by Q1?"

The CFO begins to answer, "Well, based on what we're seeing . . ." Marissa texts a pre-agreed signal to the IR head, who smoothly jumps in: "Thanks, [Analyst]. As we've said, we're encouraged by early adoption, but we're not breaking out forward projections at this time."

Later, another analyst asks, "Any reason to believe margins will expand faster than your prior 3% guidance?"

The CFO responds with his rehearsed line, "We're sticking with our prior guidance, and we'll update the market formally if it changes."

Post-Call Review

Immediately after the call, Marissa convenes a debrief.

Transcript Review. Legal and IR scrub the transcript for any loose language. One phrase—*demand looks robust*—is flagged as borderline. After discussion, they agree it's acceptable given the context, but it will be noted for next quarter's prep.

Action Items

- Legal notes that if Q4 bookings continue trending positively, the company may need to formally update guidance via 8-K or the next earnings call.
- The CEO asks for additional Q&A training before the next earnings cycle.
- Marissa agrees to lead a new media-and-disclosure bootcamp.

Lessons Reinforced

1. **Stick to the Script.** Without a disciplined script and rehearsal, the CFO would likely have implied a change to forward guidance, potentially triggering an SEC inquiry or class action if expectations weren't met.

2. **No Off-the-Cuff Guidance.** Marissa's early intervention on speculative language saved the company from disclosing MNPI without proper documentation or safe harbor protection.

3. Control the Q&A. Real-time monitoring, pre-planned redirection, and practiced deflection techniques prevented slips that could violate Reg FD or mislead investors.

Key Takeaway

In the post-call reflection, Marissa reminds the executive team that *Earnings calls aren't just investor theater; they're potential deposition transcripts. Every word matters.*

And next quarter, no one will question why Legal has a seat at the earnings table.

Final Thought: How to Stay on Regulators' Good Side

Be Proactive
If a regulatory issue is brewing, fix it before they find it. Conduct regular internal audits to identify and address potential compliance issues.

Treat Compliance as a Business Priority
It's not just a legal issue; it's a company-wide responsibility. Foster a culture of compliance throughout the organization.

Engage in Regular Compliance Training and Audits to Avoid Surprises
Provide regular training to employees on relevant laws and regulations.

Be Transparent and Cooperative
If a regulator contacts you, do not hide the ball or give the appearance that you have something to hide. Work with the regulators to answer their questions and provide the documents they want to review. Being transparent and cooperative allows you to advocate for your client's interests and provide context for your client's actions or inaction. This may find receptive ears versus falling on deaf ears if you stonewall the regulators.

Build Relationships with Regulators
Get to know the regulators who oversee your industry and build relationships based on trust and respect.

EIGHT

GLADIATOR MODE

—

NAVIGATING SHAREHOLDER ACTIVISM,
PROXY BATTLES, AND TAKEOVERS

Gladiator Mode—Navigating Shareholder Activism, Proxy Battles, and Takeovers

So, your company is under siege. Now what? You knew this day might come. Maybe it started with an innocuous Form 13D filing—a hedge fund suddenly acquiring a sizable stake in your company. Or perhaps an aggressive shareholder letter landed on the CEO's desk, packed with complaints about strategy, governance, or executive compensation. Then came the whispers of a proxy battle. Now, your company is officially "in play."

Welcome to the world of shareholder activism, proxy fights, and hostile takeovers—a part of the modern corporate landscape. This is high-stakes, full-contact corporate governance with battles for control, strategy, and vision. Winning requires preparation, discipline, and a keen understanding of governance, law, and market dynamics.

The board is looking to you, the General Counsel, to steady the ship. As GC, you are the strategist, the protector, and—when necessary—the enforcer. Your ability to anticipate threats, fortify defenses, and navigate high-stakes negotiations will determine whether your company emerges stronger or falls to outside forces—dismantled piece by piece. Forward

No pressure, right?

Here's how you navigate the storm.

Recognizing the Early Warning Signs of an Activist Investor

Activist investors don't show up overnight. They circle, they probe, they test vulnerabilities. Your job is to spot the warning signs before they become full-blown crises. Here's what to watch for:

Unusual Trading Activity
A surge in stock purchases from previously unknown entities, often structured to avoid immediate disclosure thresholds. This could indicate an activist building a position stealthily. Keep a close eye on trading volumes and patterns, especially around key corporate events or announcements.

13D Filings
A public filing by an investor acquiring 5% or more of a company's shares with the intent to influence management. This is the canary in the coal mine. The 13D filing is a clear signal that an investor has taken a significant stake and may be planning to push for changes. Monitor these filings regularly and analyze the language used in the "Purpose of Transaction" section for clues about the investor's intentions.

Shareholder Letters & Public Campaigns
Activists rarely start by knocking on the boardroom door. They begin with public criticism—letters to management, op-eds, media interviews, and social media campaigns to rally investor support. These public statements are designed to put pressure on management and garner support from other shareholders. Pay attention to the specific demands and rhetoric used, as they often foreshadow the activist's strategy.

Private Equity or Hedge Fund Accumulations
Activists often team up with institutional investors or private equity firms looking for a fast return through major strategic shifts, divestitures, or leadership changes. These partnerships can significantly amplify the activist's influence and resources. Monitor for unusual collaborations or coordinated voting patterns among seemingly unrelated investors.

Boardroom Whisper Campaigns

Activists will court your largest institutional shareholders behind the scenes, making their case before they go public. This strategy allows them to build a coalition of support before launching a more visible campaign. Maintain open lines of communication with your major shareholders to stay ahead of these efforts.

Pressure for Governance Changes

Activists may start with demands for board refreshment, changes to executive compensation, or governance modifications before escalating to an outright takeover attempt. These initial requests can be a way to test the company's responsiveness and identify potential weaknesses. Be prepared to justify your current governance practices and have a clear rationale for any areas that deviate from best practices.

Shareholder Sentiment Analysis

Implement tools to monitor social media, investor forums, and financial news outlets for shifts in shareholder sentiment. This can provide early indications of dissatisfaction that might lead to activist involvement.

Proxy Voting Trends

Analyze historical proxy voting patterns of your major shareholders. Look for changes in voting behavior that might signal growing discontent or alignment with activist positions.

Industry Comparison

Regularly benchmark your company's performance, governance practices, and shareholder returns against peers. Activists often target underperformers within an industry.

Defense Strategies Every GC Should Know

You wouldn't walk into a courtroom unprepared, and you certainly shouldn't go into a proxy battle without a plan. There are four key defenses every General Counsel needs in their arsenal.

1. Fortify Your Governance Framework
Your company's corporate bylaws and governance documents are your first line of defense. Review them now, before you need them. Ensure they include:

Staggered Board Provisions
Prevents activists from replacing the entire board in a single election cycle. This structure, also known as a classified board, divides directors into classes with staggered terms, making it more difficult for an activist to gain control quickly. However, be aware that many institutional investors view staggered boards negatively, so be prepared to justify this structure if challenged.

Advance Notice Bylaws
Requires activists to disclose their nominations well in advance, giving you time to respond. These provisions typically set deadlines for shareholders to submit proposals or director nominations, providing management with crucial preparation time. Ensure these bylaws are clear, reasonable, and consistently enforced to avoid legal challenges.

Poison Pills (Shareholder Rights Plans)
A legal mechanism that dilutes an activist's stake if they cross a certain threshold (often 10-15%), making a hostile takeover prohibitively expensive. While controversial, poison pills can be an effective deterrent against unwanted takeovers. However, they should be used judiciously and with a clear rationale, as they can face significant shareholder opposition.

Supermajority Voting Requirements
Raising the threshold for certain actions can make it harder for activists to push through changes. This might include requiring a higher percentage of shareholder votes for major corporate decisions or bylaw amendments. Be

cautious with this approach, as it can also make it difficult for the company to implement necessary changes in the future.

Board Refreshment

Implement a robust board evaluation and refreshment process. This can preempt activist criticism about board entrenchment or lack of relevant skills.

Lead Independent Director

If you haven't already, consider appointing a strong lead independent director. This role can be crucial in demonstrating good governance and providing a channel for shareholder concerns.

Governance Roadshows

Conduct annual governance roadshows where independent directors meet with major shareholders to discuss governance practices and address concerns.

2. Proactive Shareholder Engagement

Investor Day Events

Host regular investor days that showcase your company's strategy, leadership team, and growth initiatives. This provides a platform for direct engagement and helps build investor confidence.

One-on-One Meetings

Establish a program of regular one-on-one meetings between key executives and major shareholders. This personal touch can foster loyalty and provide early warning of concerns.

Shareholder Surveys

Conduct annual anonymous surveys of your shareholder base to gauge satisfaction and identify potential areas of concern before they escalate.

3. Build a War Chest & Strategic Alliances

Know Your Shareholder Base
Activists don't win alone. They need support from institutional investors. You need to be ahead of the curve, regularly engaging with key shareholders before an activist gets to them. Maintain an up-to-date understanding of your shareholder composition, including their voting histories and investment philosophies. Develop a comprehensive shareholder engagement program that includes regular communication and feedback mechanisms.

Secure Friendly Investors
If an activist shows up, you'll need a coalition of supportive shareholders who believe in management's strategy. Cultivate relationships with long-term investors who align with your company's vision and strategy. Consider reaching out to former shareholders who have sold their stakes to understand their reasoning and address any concerns they may have had.

Liquidity & Buyback Strategies
Having cash on hand or initiating stock buybacks can help stabilize share price volatility and reduce the activist's influence. A strong balance sheet can provide flexibility in responding to activist demands or market pressures. However, be prepared to justify the use of capital for buybacks versus other strategic investments or returns to shareholders.

4. Control the Narrative

Engage Early
If an activist surfaces, don't go radio silent. Proactively communicate the company's long-term strategy and governance stability. Early engagement can help shape the narrative and demonstrate management's responsiveness to shareholder concerns. Develop a clear, concise message that articulates your company's value proposition and strategic direction.

PR & Legal Coordination
Activists win by controlling the media. Ensure your legal and PR teams are aligned on messaging to counteract negative narratives. Develop a clear, consistent communication strategy that addresses potential activist critiques.

Prepare a crisis communication plan that outlines roles, responsibilities, and approval processes for rapid response to activist claims.

Prepare for the Public Fight
Activists will take their campaign to the press, investors, and proxy advisors. Be ready to tell your side of the story with facts, performance metrics, and a compelling vision for the company's future. This may include preparing detailed investor presentations, engaging with financial media, and conducting targeted outreach to key stakeholders. Consider creating a dedicated microsite or investor portal to house your rebuttals and supporting materials.

Crisis Communication Plan
Develop a detailed crisis communication plan specifically for activist situations. This should include pre-approved messaging, designated spokespersons, and a clear chain of command for decision-making.

Digital Strategy
Enhance your digital presence with a robust investor relations website and active social media engagement. Be prepared to counter activist narratives quickly across all platforms.

Employee Communications
Don't forget internal stakeholders. Develop a plan to keep employees informed and engaged during activist situations to maintain morale and productivity.

Mergers & Acquisitions: What You Need to Know When the Company Is in Play

When a company becomes a takeover target, everything changes. The stakes rise, and every decision—every word—matters. Here's how to handle a Mergers and Acquisitions (M&A) situation like a seasoned GC.

Negotiation Tactics

BATNA Development. Clearly define your Best Alternative to a Negotiated Agreement (BATNA). This strengthens your negotiating position and helps avoid reactive decision-making.

Negotiation Team Structure. Establish a core negotiation team with clearly defined roles. Consider including both internal executives and external advisors for a balanced perspective.

Deal Protection Measures. Understand the range of deal protection measures available (e.g., break-up fees, no-shop provisions) and their implications. Be prepared to negotiate these terms strategically.

Due Diligence in M&A Situations

Comprehensive Valuation Analysis. Conduct thorough internal and external valuations using multiple methodologies. Be prepared to justify your company's standalone value in detail.

Synergy Assessment. If considering a merger, perform a detailed synergy analysis. Understand not just potential cost savings, but also revenue synergies and implementation risks.

Cultural Fit Evaluation. Assess the cultural compatibility between your company and potential acquirers or merger partners. Cultural clashes can derail even the most financially sound deals.

Dos And Don'ts

Do: Control the Information Flow

Limit access to sensitive financial and strategic information. A leak can drive up the bidder's price or, worse, invite rival bids. Implement strict confidentiality protocols and consider using code names for the project. Establish a clear chain of custody for all deal-related documents and implement a secure virtual data room for sharing sensitive information with authorized parties.

Establish a dedicated response team—including Legal, Financial, PR, and Investor Relations—to ensure a coordinated response. This team should meet regularly to assess the situation and adjust strategies as needed. Develop clear communication protocols and decision-making processes to enable rapid responses to new developments.

Maintain confidentiality in board discussions. Loose lips sink deals—and sometimes entire companies. Remind directors of their fiduciary duties and the importance of discretion. Consider implementing a board portal or secure communication platform to minimize the risk of information leaks.

Do: Keep the Board Focused on Fiduciary Duties

The board—not just management—has a duty to act in the best interests of shareholders. Ensure they evaluate all options objectively. This may include considering alternative transactions or strategic alternatives that could deliver greater shareholder value. Provide regular updates to the board on market conditions, peer company performance, and industry trends to inform its decision-making.

If a deal is in play, establish a Special Committee of Independent Directors. This committee should oversee negotiations and protect against conflicts of interest. It should have its own legal and financial advisors to ensure independent analysis. Clearly define the committee's mandate, authority, and reporting requirements to the full board.

Do: Stay on Top of Regulatory Approvals (SEC, FTC, DOJ)

Antitrust concerns can derail even the best deals. Conduct a thorough antitrust analysis early in the process and be prepared to address potential regulatory hurdles. Develop a comprehensive regulatory strategy, including potential divestitures or operational changes that may be required to secure approvals.

Don't: Dismiss a Bid Too Quickly

Knee-jerk rejections can be seen as entrenchment. Consider every offer carefully and document a thorough review process to avoid breach of fiduciary duty claims. The board should be able to demonstrate that it acted in good faith and in the best interests of shareholders. Develop a clear framework for evaluating offers, including financial, strategic, and operational considerations.

Don't: Make Promises to Employees or Investors Before a Deal Is Finalized

Mergers bring uncertainty—don't add to it with premature statements. Maintain a consistent message that prioritizes shareholder value while acknowledging other stakeholders' concerns. Prepare a comprehensive communication plan for various scenarios, including deal announcement, rejection, or a protracted negotiation process.

Don't: Let emotions Dictate Strategy.

Hostile takeovers feel personal, but decisions must be made in the best interest of shareholders. Focus on objective analysis and valuation metrics rather than personal feelings or legacy considerations. Consider engaging independent financial and legal advisors to provide unbiased assessments of offers and strategic alternatives.

Don't: Underestimate the Importance of Proxy Advisors

Firms like ISS and Glass Lewis have enormous sway over institutional investors. A negative recommendation from them can tilt the outcome of a proxy fight or merger vote. Engage with proxy advisory firms early to understand their concerns and perspectives. Be prepared to address any governance or performance issues they may raise in their reports. **Engage proxy advisors early**—don't wait until the vote is imminent. Provide clear, data-driven arguments supporting the company's position. Be prepared to address any governance or performance issues they may raise. Develop a targeted outreach strategy for each major proxy advisory firm, tailoring your message to their specific methodologies and focus areas.

Don't: Assume Retail Investors Will Vote in Your Favor

Educate them on the risks and benefits of any deal. Develop targeted communication strategies for different shareholder segments, including retail investors who may require more simplified explanations of complex transactions. Consider using social media, investor webinars, or dedicated retail investor hotlines to reach this important constituency.

The Evolving Landscape of Shareholder Activism

Shareholder activism has become an increasingly prominent feature of the corporate landscape, with significant implications for companies across various sectors. Understanding the current trends and dynamics of activism is crucial for effective defense and strategic planning.

Rise of ESG Activism

Environmental, social, and governance (ESG) issues have become a focal point for many activist campaigns. Investors are increasingly pushing companies to address climate change, improve diversity and inclusion, and enhance corporate governance practices. This shift reflects broader societal concerns and the growing recognition that ESG factors can materially impact a company's long-term value and risk profile.

ESG Integration Strategy. Develop a comprehensive plan for integrating ESG factors into your business strategy and operations. This should go beyond surface-level initiatives to demonstrate genuine commitment.

ESG Reporting Framework. Adopt a recognized ESG reporting framework (e.g., SASB, GRI) to enhance transparency and comparability of your ESG efforts.

ESG-Linked Compensation. Consider tying executive compensation to ESG metrics to demonstrate alignment with long-term sustainability goals.

Key Takeaways

- Develop and communicate a clear ESG strategy aligned with your business objectives. Ensure that your ESG initiatives are integrated into your overall corporate strategy and have measurable goals and metrics.
- Regularly assess and report on ESG metrics to demonstrate progress and commitment. Consider adopting recognized reporting frameworks such as SASB or TCFD to enhance credibility and comparability.
- Be prepared to engage with investors on specific ESG issues and how they relate to long-term value creation. Develop a comprehensive

ESG engagement strategy that includes proactive outreach to key stakeholders and clear communication of your ESG priorities and progress.

Recent data from The Conference Board indicates that the number of anti-ESG proposals more than quadrupled in the Russell 3000 from 23 in 2021 to 112 in 2024, with this trend expected to intensify in 2025. This surge in anti-ESG activism highlights the need for companies to carefully balance their ESG initiatives with potential legal and financial risks, and to be prepared to defend their ESG strategies against both pro- and anti-ESG activists.

Technological Disruption and Activism

As technology continues to reshape industries, activists are increasingly targeting companies they perceive as slow to adapt to digital transformation or emerging competitive threats. This trend has been particularly pronounced in sectors like retail, media, and financial services.

Digital Transformation Roadmap

Create and communicate a clear digital transformation strategy. This should outline how you're leveraging technologies like AI, blockchain, and IoT to drive growth and efficiency.

Innovation Metrics

Develop and report on key innovation metrics (e.g., R&D spend as a percentage of revenue, new product revenue contribution) to demonstrate your commitment to staying ahead of disruption.

Tech-Savvy Board Members

Actively recruit board members with deep technology expertise to enhance oversight of digital initiatives and emerging tech risks.

Strategic Responses

- Regularly review and update your digital strategy and innovation initiatives. Establish a clear governance structure for overseeing technological innovation and digital transformation efforts.
- Consider appointing board members with relevant technological expertise. Ensure that your board has the necessary skills and knowledge to effectively oversee and guide the company's technology strategy.
- Be prepared to articulate how your technology investments and digital initiatives support long-term growth and competitiveness. Develop clear metrics and KPIs to measure the success and ROI of your digital transformation efforts.

Collaborative Activism

There's a growing trend of activists working together or partnering with institutional investors to amplify their influence. These collaborations can take various forms, from informal information sharing to formal joint ventures.

Shareholder Collaboration Monitoring. Implement advanced analytics tools to identify potential collaborations between shareholders. Look for patterns in voting behavior or public statements that might indicate coordinated efforts.

Engagement Strategy Segmentation. Develop tailored engagement strategies for different types of investors (e.g., index funds, hedge funds, pension funds), recognizing their unique priorities and decision-making processes.

Coalition Building. Proactively build relationships with long-term-oriented shareholders who can serve as allies in the event of an activist campaign.

Defensive Measures

Monitor shareholder communications and filings for signs of collaborative efforts. Utilize advanced analytics and AI-powered tools to identify patterns and relationships among your shareholders.

Develop strategies for engaging with different types of investor groups, recognizing their diverse priorities and perspectives. Tailor your engagement approach based on the specific concerns and investment strategies of each major shareholder group.

Consider building alliances with long-term institutional investors who support your strategic vision. Cultivate relationships with key institutional investors through regular, transparent communication and by demonstrating a clear link between your strategy and long-term value creation.

Five-Point Framework for General Counsel to Strategically Handle Shareholder Activism, Proxy Battles, and Takeovers

1. Detect Early: Deploy Intelligence & Surveillance Systems

Objective. Anticipate threats before they escalate.

Trading Surveillance. Monitor unusual share accumulations just below reporting thresholds.

Filing Review. Track SEC filings (13D, 13F) and decode activist language for intent.

Sentiment Analysis. Use AI tools to flag shifts in shareholder sentiment, media narratives, or social media activity.

Shareholder Mapping. Track alliances or coordinated behavior among investors—watch for quiet coalitions.

Benchmarking. Regularly compare performance, governance, and returns to peers to identify vulnerabilities activists may exploit.

Think of this phase as reconnaissance. Miss the signs, and you'll be fighting blind.

2. Fortify Defenses: Harden Governance and Legal Structures

Objective: make it legally and procedurally harder for activists to gain control.

Review Bylaws. Implement staggered boards, advance notice bylaws, and supermajority voting provisions.

Prepare a Poison Pill. Have a rights plan on standby—ready to adopt if accumulation accelerates.

Board Evaluation & Refreshment. Continually enhance board diversity, skills, and independence.

Lead Independent Director Role. Empower as a liaison to shareholders and a symbol of strong governance.

Governance Roadshows. Let independent directors engage directly with top shareholders before a crisis hits.

This is your legal armor. Weak governance invites attack—strong governance deters it.

3. Engage Strategically: Segment and Cultivate Shareholder Relationships

Objective: build trust and form coalitions before an activist does.

Engagement Segmentation. Tailor your approach for hedge funds, pension funds, index funds, and retail investors.

Major Investor Outreach. Maintain regular dialogue and anticipate concerns.

Investor Days & One-on-Ones. Create platforms to explain strategy and hear shareholder priorities.

Shareholder Surveys. Use feedback loops to detect discontent early.

Coalition Building. Identify and cultivate long-term shareholders as allies in a fight.

If you haven't built the relationship before the fire drill, don't expect to win allies during one.

4. Control the Narrative: Master Communications & Media

Objective: shape perception and defend the company's strategy in the court of public opinion.

Unified Messaging. Align legal, IR, and PR teams with pre-approved scripts and rapid-response protocols.

Microsites & Digital Strategy. Use dedicated online platforms to house rebuttals, performance data, and vision.

Internal Comms. Keep employees aligned and calm—activist pressure breeds internal uncertainty.

Proxy Advisory Firm Engagement. Meet ISS and Glass Lewis early. Don't wait until after their recommendations are published.

Activists win with stories. If you're not telling yours, someone else is telling theirs.

5. Prepare for the Fight: Activate the Legal and Strategic Command Center

Objective: execute a disciplined, cross-functional defense and M&A readiness plan.

Crisis Response Team. Assemble legal, PR, financial, and regulatory advisors with clear roles.

Negotiation Readiness. Define your BATNA, identify strategic alternatives, and prepare valuation materials.

Special Committees. Use independent directors to assess deals and avoid conflict-of-interest claims.

Deal Defense Protocols. Prepare for hostile bids with secure data rooms, confidentiality policies, and clear communication paths.

Regulatory & Proxy Planning. Understand antitrust risks and tailor strategies for both institutional and retail investor votes.

Case Studies

Scenario I: The GC Deploys Early Warning Signs to Detect an Activist Investor

You are the General Counsel (GC) of a publicly traded consumer products company. After attending a recent governance seminar, you decide to strengthen your company's defenses against activist investors by proactively deploying a suite of early warning indicators.

Deploying Trading Surveillance

You instruct your legal and compliance teams to enhance monitoring of daily trading volumes and patterns. You set up alerts for any unusual trading activity, particularly spikes in purchases by previously unknown entities or patterns that suggest accumulation just below the 5% disclosure threshold.

> **Result.** Within days, your system flags a cluster of new institutional buyers each acquiring 4.8% of shares. You immediately escalate this to your executive team, highlighting the potential for stealth activist accumulation.

Monitoring 13D Filings

You assign a junior attorney to review all new SEC Schedule 13D filings daily, focusing on any that mention your company. You also request a summary of the "Purpose of Transaction" sections for any filings that cross the 5% threshold.

> **Result.** A 13D filing appears from a hedge fund, stating its intent to "engage with management regarding strategic alternatives." You circulate an internal memo alerting leadership to the risk of an activist campaign.

Scanning for Public Campaigns

You deploy a media monitoring tool to track shareholder letters, op-eds, and social media mentions of your company. You also monitor financial news outlets for any critical commentary.

> **Result.** The tool picks up a critical letter from the hedge fund, published in a major business journal, followed by a flurry of negative social media posts. You share these findings with investor relations and recommend preparing a public response.

Watching for Unusual Investor Alliances

You ask your corporate secretary to analyze recent 13F filings and proxy voting records for signs of coordinated voting or share accumulation by private equity firms or hedge funds.

> **Result.** You discover that a private equity firm has started buying shares shortly after the hedge fund's 13D filing. You flag this as a potential alliance and recommend a board-level discussion about possible coordinated action.

Engaging with Major Shareholders

You personally reach out to your largest institutional investors, asking if they've been approached by any activist investors or have concerns about governance.

> **Result.** Several investors confirm private conversations with the hedge fund. You use this intelligence to brief the CEO and board, emphasizing the need for proactive engagement with these key shareholders.

Ongoing: Sentiment and Proxy Analysis

You implement a real-time sentiment analysis dashboard for social media and investor forums, and commission a report on proxy voting trends among your top 10 shareholders.

> **Result.** Both tools reveal growing shareholder dissatisfaction and a shift in voting patterns away from management. You use this data to prepare a shareholder engagement plan and recommend governance enhancements.

Benchmarking and Board Preparation

You direct your team to benchmark your company's governance practices and performance against industry peers, preparing a gap analysis for the next board meeting.

> **Result.** You identify several areas for improvement and draft a communication plan to address them before the activist can use them as leverage.

Through the proactive deployment of early warning systems and vigilant monitoring, the GC has positioned the company to identify and respond swiftly to the evolving threat of activist investor activity. By integrating trading surveillance, regulatory filing reviews, media monitoring, and direct shareholder engagement, the legal team has not only detected stealth accumulation and coordinated investor actions but also provided timely intelligence to leadership and the board.

These actions have enabled the company to anticipate activist tactics, prepare tailored shareholder communications, and benchmark governance practices for continuous improvement. Ultimately, this comprehensive and coordinated approach demonstrates the critical role of the General Counsel in safeguarding corporate stability, influencing business strategy, and ensuring the company remains one step ahead in the face of activist pressure.

Scenario II: The General Counsel's Proxy Battle Playbook in Action
Imagine a mid-sized public technology company, TechNova Inc., suddenly finds itself the target of an activist investor group, Starboard Equity, which is dissatisfied with the company's strategic direction and seeks to replace most of the board. As General Counsel (GC), you must deploy every defensive tool in your arsenal to protect the company's governance, reputation, and long-term strategy.

Fortify the Governance Framework
Months before any activist surfaced, you led a review of TechNova's bylaws and ensured the board was classified, so only a third of directors are up for election each year. This structure now prevents Starboard from replacing the entire board in one cycle, buying you critical time.

Your bylaws require shareholders to submit board nominations 90 days before the annual meeting. When Starboard tries to nominate directors, you quickly verify their compliance with these deadlines, giving management time to prepare a robust response.

With Starboard's stake nearing 10%, you recommend that the board adopt a "just-in-case" poison pill, ready to dilute any hostile accumulation of shares if the threshold is crossed.

Major bylaw changes and board removals require a two-thirds shareholder vote, making it harder for Starboard to push through sweeping changes without broad support.

Anticipating activist scrutiny, you had already instituted annual board evaluations, leading to the recent addition of two directors with digital transformation expertise, undercutting Starboard's claims of board stagnation.

You ensured a respected, independent director is in place, serving as a shareholder liaison and demonstrating governance best practices.

Months before the fight, you organized governance roadshows where independent directors met top institutional investors, gathering feedback and building trust.

Proactive Shareholder Engagement
- You schedule an emergency investor day to showcase TechNova's turnaround plan and highlight recent wins, providing a platform for management to address concerns directly.

- Your IR team, with your guidance, holds a series of private calls with major shareholders to listen to their concerns and explain why supporting the current board is in their best interest.
- You distribute an anonymous survey to gauge investor sentiment, quickly identifying and addressing key issues before Starboard can exploit them.

Build a War Chest & Strategic Alliances

- You maintain a detailed database of shareholder profiles, voting histories, and investment philosophies, allowing you to anticipate which investors might side with Starboard and which are likely to support management.
- Leveraging long-standing relationships, you reach out to supportive institutional investors, securing public statements of confidence in the current board and management.
- With a strong balance sheet, you advise the board to announce a moderate share buyback, signaling confidence in the company's future and reducing the activist's relative influence.

Control the Narrative

- As soon as Starboard's intentions become public, you coordinate a rapid response, issuing a press release that outlines the company's long-term vision and recent governance improvements.
- You assemble a cross-functional defense team—legal, PR, IR, and outside advisors—to ensure all messaging is unified and legally sound.
- Anticipating a media blitz, you prepare detailed investor presentations, fact sheets, and FAQs, and launch a dedicated microsite debunking Starboard's claims with data and case studies.
- Your pre-approved crisis plans kick in, with clear roles for spokespeople and a rapid approval chain for all public statements.
- You bolster TechNova's investor relations website and social media presence, ensuring swift, accurate responses to any misinformation.
- You send regular internal updates, reassuring employees about the company's stability and vision, maintaining morale and productivity throughout the campaign.

The proxy battle at TechNova Inc. demonstrates the critical, multifaceted role of the General Counsel in safeguarding corporate governance, aligning legal strategy with business objectives, and protecting the company's long-term interests. By proactively strengthening the governance framework through staggered board terms, robust bylaw provisions, and independent director engagement, you created structural defenses that blunted Starboard Equity's immediate impact and signaled a commitment to best practices. Strategic, transparent shareholder engagement and the cultivation of institutional support not only built trust but also ensured that management's vision resonated with key stakeholders, mitigating the activist's narrative. Your orchestration of a unified, rapid-response communications plan preserved TechNova's reputation and employee morale, while tactical financial moves further reinforced confidence in the company's future. Ultimately, this scenario underscores how a vigilant, well-prepared General Counsel can turn a proxy contest into an opportunity to showcase sound governance, reinforce board relationships, and advance the company's strategic agenda in the face of external pressure.

Scenario III: M&A in Play—Navigating a High-Stakes Takeover as Vice President of Legal

You are the vice president of Legal at a publicly traded technology company. Rumors have surfaced that a major competitor is preparing a takeover bid. The board is on high alert, and the CEO has tasked you with safeguarding the company's interests while preparing for a critical strategy session with the Chief of Staff. Your priorities are to protect sensitive information, maintain board cohesion, and ensure the company's legal and strategic posture is robust.

The Situation Unfolds

Information Control and Confidentiality. As news of the potential takeover circulates, you immediately implement strict confidentiality protocols:

- Limit access to sensitive financial and strategic documents, using code names for the project and a secure virtual data room for authorized sharing.
- Establish a clear chain of custody for all deal-related materials, ensuring only essential personnel have access.
- Remind the board and executive team of their fiduciary duties and the critical importance of discretion, leveraging a secure board portal for all communications.

Forming the Response and Negotiation Teams. You convene a dedicated response team comprising legal, financial, PR, and investor relations experts. This group meets daily to:

- Monitor developments and adjust strategies in real time.
- Develop clear communication protocols and rapid decision-making processes.
- Assemble a core negotiation team, including both internal executives and external advisors, with clearly defined roles and responsibilities.

You also ensure the company's BATNA (best alternative to a negotiated agreement) is thoroughly developed, so the board is never forced into reactive decision-making.

Due Diligence and Deal Assessment. With the board's support, you oversee:
- a comprehensive internal and external valuation using multiple methodologies to justify the company's stand-alone value
- synergy analysis to assess both cost savings and revenue opportunities, as well as cultural compatibility with the potential acquirer
- a rigorous review of deal protection measures (e.g., break-up fees, no-shop provisions), preparing to negotiate these terms strategically

Board Governance and Fiduciary Focus. You reinforce the board's duty to act in shareholders' best interests, not just that of management. To ensure objectivity and independence:
- A Special Committee of Independent Directors is established, with its own legal and financial advisors, to oversee negotiations and guard against conflicts of interest.
- The committee's mandate, authority, and reporting requirements are clearly defined.
- Regular updates are provided on market conditions, peer performance, and industry trends to inform decision-making.

You also initiate early engagement with regulatory counsel to prepare for potential antitrust reviews and other regulatory hurdles.

Communication and Stakeholder Management. You coordinate with the PR and investor relations teams to:
- Develop a comprehensive communication plan for various scenarios: deal announcement, rejection, or protracted negotiations.
- Maintain a consistent message that prioritizes shareholder value while acknowledging employee and investor concerns.
- Avoid making premature promises to employees or investors, instead preparing clear, data-driven messaging for all stakeholder groups.

Proxy Advisors and Retail Investors. Recognizing the influence of proxy advisory firms, you:
- Engage with ISS and Glass Lewis early, providing transparent, data-driven arguments to support the company's position.
- Prepare targeted outreach strategies for each major proxy advisor, addressing any governance or performance issues they may raise.

- Launch educational campaigns for retail investors, using webinars, social media, and hotlines to explain the risks and benefits of the deal in accessible terms.

Key Takeaways

Do:

- Rigorously control information flow and access.
- Build a multidisciplinary response team with clear protocols.
- Keep the board focused on fiduciary duties and independent oversight.
- Engage early with regulators and proxy advisors.
- Communicate consistently and transparently with all stakeholders.

Don't:

- Dismiss bids without thorough, documented review.
- Make premature promises or statements to employees or investors.
- Let emotions or personal interests drive strategy.
- Underestimate the influence of proxy advisors or retail investors.

Navigating a high-stakes M&A scenario requires a disciplined, strategic approach that balances confidentiality, stakeholder communication, and rigorous board oversight. By proactively controlling information, assembling a skilled response team, and engaging with key advisors and stakeholders, the company not only protects its interests but also demonstrates strong governance and commitment to shareholder value. This careful orchestration of legal, financial, and operational strategies positions the company to respond effectively to any offer, whether that means negotiating favorable terms, pursuing alternative transactions, or standing firm against undervalued bids. Ultimately, the company emerges from the process with its reputation intact, its options open, and its leadership trusted by both the board and shareholders.

Scenario IV Response: A Proactive and Robust Approach to Shareholder Activism

In 2025, Acme Corp., a leading industrial company, is at the center of escalating shareholder activism focused on ESG (environmental, social, and governance) issues. The company has already taken significant steps to integrate ESG into its strategy, adopting the SASB framework and tying executive compensation to ESG performance. However, with anti-ESG proposals in the Russell 3000 quadrupling from 2021 to 2024 and further intensification expected, Acme faces simultaneous pressure from both pro- and anti-ESG activist groups.

Situation

At its upcoming annual meeting, Acme must address:
- Pro-ESG Activists. Demanding accelerated climate action, greater board diversity, and transparent supply chain practices.
- Anti-ESG Activists. Urging a rollback of ESG initiatives, citing resource diversion and increased legal/financial risks.

Proactive and Robust Strategic Response

1. Deepen Board Engagement and Alignment
- Conduct a dedicated board strategy session to review the evolving activism landscape, ensuring all directors are aligned on the company's ESG vision and prepared to respond cohesively to both pro- and anti-ESG pressures.
- Provide the board with scenario analyses and legal briefings on potential outcomes of activist proposals, enabling informed, unified decision-making.

2. Advance ESG Integration Beyond Compliance
- Launch a company-wide ESG innovation task force, empowering cross-functional leaders to identify new opportunities for ESG-driven value creation, such as green product lines or sustainable supply chain partnerships.
- Set ambitious, science-based targets for climate and diversity, with clear timelines and public commitments, demonstrating leadership rather than mere compliance.

3. Elevate Transparency and Stakeholder Communication
- Issue quarterly ESG updates, not just annual reports, using SASB and TCFD frameworks to provide granular, comparable data on progress, setbacks, and next steps.
- Host investor roundtables and webcasts specifically focused on ESG strategy, inviting both proponents and skeptics for open dialogue and Q&A.

4. Proactively Address Anti-ESG Concerns
- Commission an independent third-party review of the financial and legal impacts of ESG initiatives, publishing the findings to demonstrate the business case and risk mitigation strategies.
- Develop a targeted communication plan for anti-ESG stakeholders, emphasizing how ESG efforts are calibrated to drive long-term value, safeguard reputation, and ensure regulatory compliance, rather than distract from core operations.

5. Strengthen Legal and Crisis Preparedness
- Assemble a rapid-response legal and communications team to monitor activist developments, anticipate new proposals, and craft tailored responses for each scenario.
- Prepare detailed legal analyses for each activist proposal, mapping out regulatory, fiduciary, and reputational risks, and ensuring all public statements are defensible and consistent with evolving law.

6. Foster a Culture of Continuous Improvement and Engagement
- Implement a feedback loop with employees, customers, and community partners to gather input on ESG priorities, ensuring that initiatives are responsive and credible.
- Regularly benchmark Acme's ESG performance against industry leaders and disclose both achievements and areas for improvement, signaling transparency and a commitment to best practices.

Acme Corp.'s proactive and comprehensive approach to the evolving landscape of shareholder activism demonstrates its commitment to long-term value creation, responsible governance, and stakeholder engagement. By anticipating challenges from both pro- and anti-ESG activists, deepening board alignment, and embracing transparency, the company not only mitigates legal and reputational risks but also sets a benchmark for industry leadership. This forward-thinking strategy positions Acme to thrive amid shifting investor expectations and regulatory demands, ensuring its resilience and competitiveness in a dynamic corporate environment.

Final Thought: This Is a Game of Chess, Not Checkers

Plan ten moves ahead, and have your queen (legal strategy) ready.

Stay Ahead of Disclosure Risks

If bad news is coming, control the messaging before the market does. Work with the investor relations team to develop a communication plan that is accurate, transparent, and timely.

Understand Activist Investors

They can shake up leadership and push for changes that affect your role. Monitor activist investor activity and be prepared to respond to their demands.

Work Closely with the IR (Investor Relations) Team to Ensure the Company's Messaging Aligns with Legal Requirements

Review all investor communications, including press releases, earnings calls, and SEC filings, to ensure that they are accurate and compliant with applicable laws and regulations.

Be Prepared to Answer Investor Questions

Be ready to answer questions from investors about legal and regulatory matters.

Build Relationships with Key Investors

Get to know the company's major investors and build relationships based on trust and transparency.

Read Analyst Reports

Investors read and many times rely on the reports prepared by analysts employed by investment banks and research houses. Therefore, so should you. Make sure you understand what the investment community is saying about your company. These reports will give you the ability to "see around corners" and allow you to help the company take advantage of tailwinds or mitigate the drag from headwinds.

NINE

CRISIS MODE

—

WHEN THINGS GO WRONG

Crisis Mode— When Things Go Wrong

If you're the General Counsel of a public company, you're also the Chief Firefighter. No matter how airtight your compliance program is, how well your company operates, or how ethical your leadership is, at some point, things *will* go wrong. A regulatory investigation. A whistleblower claim. A corporate scandal splashed across the front page of the *Wall Street Journal*. When a crisis hits, all eyes turn to you.

The difference between a contained incident and a full-blown catastrophe often comes down to how the legal team responds. This chapter will walk you through how to manage regulatory probes, corporate scandals, and internal investigations while keeping the company (and yourself) intact. We'll delve into practical steps, real-world examples, and proactive strategies to help you navigate these turbulent waters. Remember, your ability to navigate a crisis is not just about legal expertise; it's about leadership, communication, and the ability to remain calm under immense pressure.

The Evolving Landscape of Corporate Crisis

Before diving into specifics, it's crucial to acknowledge the changing nature of corporate crises. Today's crises are faster, louder, and more unforgiving. They're amplified by social media, weaponized by misinformation, and scrutinized by a public that expects real-time accountability. Crisis management now requires speed, transparency, cross-functional coordination, and above all, judgment.

The Speed of Social Media
A single tweet, a leaked video, or a viral hashtag can ignite a reputational firestorm within minutes. Traditional response timelines are obsolete. Companies must invest in social listening tools, establish rapid response protocols, and empower crisis teams to act decisively. The first statement, however brief, often frames the narrative. Silence is no longer neutral; it's interpreted as evasiveness.

Increased Stakeholder Scrutiny
Stakeholders today don't just want answers; they want values. Investors demand ESG transparency. Employees want ethical leadership. Customers vote with their wallets. The public expects social responsibility. A misstep in any of these areas can escalate a routine issue into a full-blown crisis. Companies must embed stakeholder mapping into their crisis planning to anticipate and address each audience with tailored messaging.

Globalization
Crises ignore borders. A regulatory investigation in one country can trigger probes in others. A product recall in Asia can spark lawsuits in the U.S. and media outrage in Europe. Cultural expectations vary—what reads as an acceptable apology in Tokyo may fall flat in Toronto. Legal teams must coordinate globally and understand the interplay between international law, local media environments, and regional regulatory regimes.

The Blurring Lines Between Legal and PR
A winning legal argument can be a reputational loss. Conversely, a PR win that overshares can jeopardize privilege or trigger litigation. The General Counsel must be fluent in communications risk and work arm-in-arm with public relations to craft messages that are legally sound, audience-appropriate, and reputationally strategic. Messaging should be pressure-tested across Legal, Compliance, HR, and Communications before going live.

Employee Activism and Internal Dissent

Employees are no longer silent bystanders. They blog, tweet, walk out, and leak to the press. They expect alignment between corporate values and corporate actions, and will call out hypocrisy in real time. An internal scandal or perceived inconsistency can go external in seconds. Companies must communicate authentically with their workforce during a crisis and consider internal communications as *mission-critical.*

Third-Party Risk and Supply Chain Failures

A company's reputation is only as strong as its weakest vendor. Crises now frequently originate from third parties—data breaches at vendors, labor abuses in the supply chain, or environmental violations by contractors. Due diligence, contractual risk-shifting, and crisis escalation procedures for third-party incidents must be baked into procurement and legal operations.

The Permanence of Digital Footprints

In the digital age, nothing truly disappears. A misstatement, a deleted tweet, or a half-hearted apology will live forever online. Search engines don't forgive, and screenshots don't forget. Companies must assume that every internal communication can go public and that every public statement will be dissected. Precision and clarity in communication aren't optional; they're survival tools.

Regulatory Pile-On and Multi-Front Exposure

A single triggering event—say, a whistleblower allegation or a major data breach—can attract parallel investigations from the SEC, DOJ, FTC, state AGs, and foreign regulators. Each has different priorities and timelines. The General Counsel must coordinate legal responses across multiple fronts, while also managing litigation hold notices, internal investigations, and reputational fallout—all at once.

The Rise of Deepfakes and Misinformation

Technology has introduced a new breed of reputational threat. AI-generated deepfakes, fake press releases, and misinformation campaigns can sow chaos before truth catches up. Legal and communications teams must be trained to recognize and respond to synthetic content, verify facts before reacting, and work with platforms to swiftly take down malicious content.

Litigation as a Communications Strategy
Increasingly, plaintiffs' lawyers and activists are using lawsuits as PR weapons. Filings are shared with the media before being served. Class actions are accompanied by press releases. Allegations—true or not—can shape public perception and investor sentiment. Legal strategy must account not only for courtroom success, but also the parallel court of public opinion.

Handling Regulatory Investigations, Whistleblower Claims, and Corporate Scandals

Regulators don't investigate companies for fun. If they come knocking, it means they believe there's a problem. Whether it's the SEC, DOJ, FTC, or another agency, your job is to control the process, minimize exposure, and protect the company's reputation. This requires a blend of legal acumen, strategic thinking, and crisis management skills. Remember that regulators have significant resources and the power to impose substantial penalties, so a proactive and cooperative approach is generally the best course of action.

The Regulatory Investigation Playbook
Regulatory investigations can be daunting, but a structured approach is essential. Here's a detailed playbook to guide you:

1. Don't Panic: Get the Facts.
Your initial reaction is critical. Avoid knee-jerk responses and focus on gathering information. Panic can lead to mistakes, such as premature admissions of guilt or the destruction of evidence. A calm, methodical approach is essential for navigating the initial stages of a regulatory investigation.

> **Is It a Subpoena? A Civil Investigative Demand? A Request for Information?** Understand the scope before reacting. Determine the specific legal requirements associated with each type of request. A

subpoena carries the force of law and requires a mandatory response, while a request for information may allow for more negotiation on scope and timing.

What Is the Agency Looking For? Narrow the focus to avoid over-disclosure. Identify the specific documents, data, and information that the agency is seeking. Over-disclosure can lead to unnecessary scrutiny and potentially expose the company to additional liability.

Identify Key Players Internally. Who has the information regulators want? Create a list of individuals who will be involved in the response, and their respective roles. This will help you coordinate the response effort and ensure that all relevant information is gathered and reviewed.

Analyze the Regulator's Motivation. Try to understand why the regulator is initiating the investigation. What are their specific concerns? What are they hoping to achieve? Understanding the regulator's motivation can help you tailor your response and negotiate a favorable outcome.

2. Secure Documents and Preserve Evidence.
This is paramount. Failure to preserve evidence can lead to obstruction of justice charges and significantly worsen the situation. Spoliation of evidence, whether intentional or unintentional, can have severe legal consequences.

Implement a Legal Hold Immediately to Prevent Accidental or Intentional Destruction of Records. Notify all relevant employees that they must preserve all documents and data related to the investigation, regardless of whether they believe it's relevant. This includes emails, documents, electronic files, voicemails, and even personal devices if they were used for company business.

Work with IT to Suspend Routine Data Deletions. Ensure that backup tapes are preserved and that no data is overwritten. Implement procedures to prevent the automatic deletion of emails and other electronic documents.

Communicate with Employees. No one should "clean up" emails or files. Emphasize that altering or destroying documents is illegal and can result in criminal penalties. Clearly explain the scope of the legal hold and the importance of preserving all relevant information.

Monitor Compliance. Regularly remind employees of the legal hold and monitor their compliance. Conduct periodic audits to ensure that employees are preserving documents and data as required.

Document Preservation Efforts. Maintain a detailed record of all preservation efforts, including the date and time the legal hold was implemented, the employees who were notified, and the steps taken to prevent data deletion. This documentation can be crucial in defending against claims of spoliation.

Address Personal Devices. With the increased use of personal devices for company business, ensure the legal hold extends to these devices. Provide guidance to employees on how to preserve relevant data from their personal devices.

3. Bring in Outside Counsel (Yes, Really).

Even if your internal team is strong, regulators take external counsel more seriously. Outside counsel brings specific advantages in regulatory investigations. The decision to engage outside counsel is a critical one, and it should be made early in the process.

Even if Your Internal Team Is Strong, Regulators Take External Counsel More Seriously. Regulators often view outside counsel as more objective and independent than in-house counsel. Their presence signals that the company is taking the investigation seriously.

Outside Firms Create a Buffer Between Executives and Government Investigators. Outside counsel can act as a shield, protecting executives from direct questioning and potential missteps. They can also help to manage the flow of information between the company and the government.

They Also Help Avoid Privilege Waivers. Experienced outside counsel can help protect attorney-client privilege and work product doctrine, ensuring that sensitive information remains confidential. They are experts in navigating the complex rules of privilege in the context of government investigations.

Specialized Knowledge. Choose a firm with specific expertise in the area under investigation. Securities law, antitrust, environmental regulations—each require a unique skill set.

Objectivity. Outside counsel can offer an unbiased assessment of the situation, free from internal pressures and biases.
Negotiating Experience. They are skilled negotiators who can often achieve more favorable outcomes with regulators than in-house counsel.

4. Control Internal Communications.
Employees should not engage with regulators without legal guidance. Loose lips sink ships. In a regulatory investigation, uncontrolled internal communications can be disastrous. Maintaining control over internal communications is essential for preventing the spread of misinformation and protecting the company's legal position.

Employees Should Not Engage with Regulators Without Legal Guidance. Designate a spokesperson or a small team to handle all communications related to the investigation. Instruct employees to direct all inquiries from regulators to the designated spokesperson or outside counsel.
Develop Talking Points to Prevent Off-the-Cuff, Misleading, or Contradictory Statements. Prepare clear, concise talking points for employees who may be contacted by regulators or the media. These talking points should be carefully vetted by legal counsel.
Remind Leadership That Emails and Texts Will Become Part of the Record. Emphasize to leadership that all emails, texts, and other written communications are potentially discoverable and will likely become part of the official record. Advise them to communicate cautiously and avoid speculation or admissions of wrongdoing.
Centralize Communication. Establish a clear chain of command for all communications related to the investigation. Designate a single point of contact for all inquiries from regulators, the media, and other stakeholders.
Social Media Monitoring. Monitor social media for mentions of the company and the investigation. Be prepared to respond to any false or misleading information that is being disseminated online.

Training. Provide training to employees on how to communicate effectively during a crisis. Emphasize the importance of sticking to the approved talking points and avoiding speculation.

5. Cooperate (Without Rolling Over).

Regulators appreciate responsiveness, but don't hand them more than necessary. Cooperation is generally advisable, but it must be strategic. Finding the right balance between cooperating and protecting the company's interests is one of the trickiest—and most important—challenges in any regulatory investigation.

Regulators Appreciate Responsiveness, But Don't Hand Them More than Necessary. Respond promptly to regulator requests for information. Delay or stonewalling can create a negative impression and prolong the investigation.

Be Strategic. Protect privileged documents and assert legal defenses where applicable. Provide the information requested, but don't volunteer more than necessary. Carefully review all documents before disclosure to ensure accuracy and completeness.

Protect Privileged Documents and Assert Legal Defenses. Clearly mark privileged materials and explain the legal basis. Don't waive privilege or concede liability just to appear cooperative.

If Settlement Is an Option, Weigh It against Prolonged Scrutiny and Financial Penalties. Consider cost, reputational impact, legal precedent, and business continuity when evaluating settlement options.

Document Requests. Scrutinize every request. Push back on vague, overbroad, or unduly burdensome demands.

Witness Preparation. No one walks into a regulatory interview cold. Prep witnesses on scope, expectations, and potential pitfalls.

Negotiation. Negotiate scope, production timelines, and settlement terms. Regulators expect it. Respectfully pushing back is not obstruction; it's advocacy.

Consider a White Paper. In complex matters, a well-crafted white paper can preempt enforcement by framing the facts and the law before the regulator draws conclusions.

Whistleblower Complaints: The Fastest Route to a Full-Blown Crisis

Few things trigger a corporate crisis faster than a whistleblower complaint. Once an employee blows the whistle to the SEC, DOJ, or media, you're in reactive mode. The best approach? Get ahead of it before it goes external. A robust and well-publicized internal reporting mechanism is crucial for detecting and addressing potential issues before they escalate into full-blown crises.

1. Take Every Complaint Seriously.

Treating every complaint with respect and conducting a thorough investigation is essential for maintaining employee trust and preventing potential legal and reputational damage.

Even Frivolous Claims Can Spiral if Mishandled. A dismissive attitude can fuel the whistleblower's determination to go public. Even if the complaint appears to be without merit, it's important to conduct a preliminary assessment to determine whether there is any basis for the allegations.

Assume Regulators Will See the Complaint, So Document Your Process Thoroughly. Thoroughly document your process, including the steps taken to investigate the allegations, the evidence gathered, and the conclusions reached. This documentation will be critical if the complaint is later investigated by regulators.

Maintain Confidentiality. Protect the identity of the whistleblower to the greatest extent possible. This will help to prevent retaliation and encourage other employees to come forward with information about wrongdoing.

Prompt Acknowledgment. Acknowledge receipt of the complaint promptly. This demonstrates that the company takes the complaint seriously and is committed to addressing the concerns raised.

Clear Communication Channels. Establish clear communication channels between the whistleblower and the company's investigators. This will help to ensure that the whistleblower is kept informed of the progress of the investigation and has an opportunity to provide additional information.

2. Act Fast, but Don't Overreact.
Conduct an initial credibility assessment, asking what evidence supports the allegations. A rapid and well-reasoned response is critical for containing the potential damage from a whistleblower complaint.

Conduct an Initial Credibility Assessment. What evidence supports the allegations? Determine the credibility of the allegations. Are they specific and detailed? Is there any supporting evidence?

Interview the Whistleblower Early, with Another Legal Team Member Present. This allows you to gather more information about the allegations and assess the whistleblower's motivation.

Independent Investigation. Ensure that the investigation is conducted by individuals who are independent and unbiased. Avoid using individuals who are close to the subject of the complaint.

Preserve Evidence. Take steps to preserve all relevant evidence, including documents, emails, and electronic data.

Legal Analysis. Conduct a legal analysis of the allegations to determine whether they raise any potential legal issues.

External Expertise. Consider engaging outside experts, such as forensic accountants or industry consultants, to assist with the investigation.

3. Protect Against Retaliation.
Any adverse action against the whistleblower will only escalate the situation. Retaliation against whistleblowers is illegal and can result in significant legal penalties. Creating a culture of non-retaliation is essential for encouraging employees to report wrongdoing.

Any Adverse Action Against the Whistleblower Will Only Escalate the Situation. Implement a strict zero-tolerance policy against retaliation. Any adverse action against the whistleblower will only escalate the situation and could result in legal liability.

Communicate the Policy. Clearly communicate the anti-retaliation policy to all employees and emphasize that retaliation will not be tolerated.

Monitor the Workplace. Actively monitor the whistleblower's work environment to ensure that they are not being subjected to any form of retaliation.

Training. Provide training to managers and supervisors on how to avoid retaliating against whistleblowers.

Discipline. Take disciplinary action against any employee who engages in retaliation.

Confidentiality. Protect the identity of the whistleblower to the greatest extent possible.

4. Determine if Self-Reporting Is Necessary.

Proactive reporting can mitigate penalties and preserve corporate credibility. The decision to self-report a potential violation is a complex one that should be made in consultation with outside counsel.

Proactive Reporting Can Mitigate Penalties and Preserve Corporate Credibility. If the issue is significant (e.g., fraud, FCPA violations), consider voluntary disclosure to regulators.

Consult Outside Counsel on Whether to Self-Report. Proactive reporting can mitigate penalties and preserve corporate credibility. Regulators often reward companies that come forward voluntarily with information about wrongdoing.

Weigh the Benefits and Risks. Carefully weigh the benefits and risks of self-reporting, including the potential for reduced penalties and the risk of increased scrutiny.

Prepare a Disclosure Plan. Develop a plan for making the disclosure to regulators, including the timing of the disclosure, the information to be disclosed, and the individuals who will be involved in the disclosure process.

Cooperate with Regulators. Cooperate fully with regulators throughout the investigation process.

Remediation. Take steps to remediate the underlying issues that led to the violation.

Document Everything. Document all steps taken in connection with the self-reporting process.

Corporate Scandal: The Ultimate Stress Test

When a scandal breaks, it's not just a legal issue; it's a full-blown reputational and business crisis. Your job is to contain the damage, steer the company toward resolution, and ensure leadership doesn't make things worse. Corporate scandals can have devastating consequences for a company, including loss of market share, damage to reputation, and legal liability.

1. Stabilize the Situation.
In the immediate aftermath of a scandal, it's essential to stabilize the situation and prevent further damage.

Control the Narrative. Work with PR to develop a clear, truthful message. This message should address the key allegations, outline the company's response, and reassure stakeholders that the company is taking the matter seriously.

Establish a Response Team. Legal, PR, HR, and Compliance should work in lockstep. Create a cross-functional team consisting of Legal, PR, HR, Compliance, and other relevant departments. This team should work in lockstep to coordinate the company's response.

Limit Internal Speculation. Employees need reassurance, not chaos. Remind employees that rumors and speculation can be harmful. Encourage them to direct all inquiries to the designated spokesperson.

Assess the Impact. Conduct a thorough assessment of the potential impact of the scandal on the company's operations, financial performance, and reputation.

Identify Key Stakeholders. Identify the key stakeholders who are affected by the scandal, including employees, customers, investors, and regulators.

Develop a Communication Plan. Develop a comprehensive communication plan that outlines how the company will communicate with each of its stakeholders.

2. Assess the Legal Exposure.
Identify potential legal claims (securities fraud, employment violations, regulatory breaches). A thorough assessment of the legal exposure is critical for developing an effective legal strategy.

Identify Potential Legal Claims. Identify all potential legal claims that could arise from the scandal, including securities fraud, employment violations, regulatory breaches, and contractual disputes.

Determine the Likelihood of Litigation and Regulatory Action. Consider the potential costs and risks associated with each scenario. **Prepare for Government Inquiries.** If necessary, prepare for government inquiries by gathering relevant documents and information, identifying potential witnesses, and developing a legal strategy.

Engage Outside Counsel. Engage experienced outside counsel to advise on the legal aspects of the scandal.

Conduct an Internal Investigation. Conduct an internal investigation to determine the facts and circumstances surrounding the scandal.

Assess Insurance Coverage. Assess the company's insurance coverage to determine whether any policies may cover the losses resulting from the scandal.

3. Communicate Wisely: Both Internally and Externally
Internal emails will be subpoenaed, so assume everything will become public. Effective communication is essential for managing the reputational and legal risks associated with a corporate scandal.

Internal Emails Will Be Subpoenaed. Assume everything will become public. Advise them to communicate cautiously and avoid making any statements that could be misinterpreted or used against the company.

Leadership Should Stick to Prepared Statements. No improvisation. Off-the-cuff remarks can create additional liability and damage the company's reputation.

Work with PR. Ensure that all messaging is consistent with the company's legal strategy and does not create additional liability.

Be Transparent. Be as transparent as possible with stakeholders, while also protecting the company's legal position.

Be Consistent. Ensure that all communications are consistent with the company's overall message.

Be Timely. Respond to inquiries from stakeholders in a timely manner.

Monitor Media Coverage. Monitor media coverage of the scandal and be prepared to correct any false or misleading information.

Develop a Social Media Strategy. Develop a social media strategy to address the scandal and protect the company's reputation online.

How to Avoid (or Manage) a PR Nightmare

The legal team must work together with PR. A poorly handled crisis can cost more in reputational damage than in legal fines. A proactive and coordinated approach to crisis communication is essential for protecting the company's reputation and minimizing the potential damage from a crisis.

Crisis Communication Rules for GCs

Truth Beats Spin. A misleading statement today becomes a scandal tomorrow. Transparency and honesty are crucial for building trust with stakeholders.

Speed Matters. If you don't control the narrative, someone else will. Respond quickly and proactively to address rumors and misinformation.

Every Word Counts. Assume the press, regulators, and plaintiffs' lawyers will dissect every statement. Carefully craft your messaging to avoid creating additional liability.

Apologize When Necessary. A genuine acknowledgment of mistakes can prevent further damage. An apology demonstrates empathy and a willingness to take responsibility.

Prepare for Leaks. Assume internal emails and memos will be exposed. Write accordingly. Avoid using inflammatory language or making statements that could be easily misconstrued.

Consistency. Ensure that all communications are consistent across all channels.

Empathy. Show empathy for those who have been affected by the crisis.

Responsibility. Take responsibility for the company's actions.

Action. Outline the steps that the company is taking to address the crisis.

Social Media: Where Corporate Nightmares Live

Monitor discussions in real time. Negative press spreads faster than ever. Social media has become a powerful force in shaping public opinion and can quickly amplify a crisis. Companies must have a social media crisis communication plan in place to respond effectively to online threats.

Monitor Discussions in Real Time. Negative press spreads faster than ever. Use social listening tools to track mentions of your company and identify potential crises.

Ensure Leadership Isn't Making Things Worse. One rogue tweet can tank stock prices. Remind executives to think before they post and to avoid engaging in online arguments.

Coordinate Social Media Responses with PR and Legal. Every post must align with legal strategy. Develop a social media crisis communication plan that outlines who is responsible for responding to inquiries and what types of messages should be used.

Identify Key Influencers. Identify the key influencers who are talking about your company on social media.

Engage with Influencers. Engage with influencers to correct misinformation and share your company's perspective.

Respond to Negative Comments. Respond to negative comments and address concerns in a timely and professional manner.

Use Visuals. Use visuals, such as images and videos, to communicate your message effectively.

Be Authentic. Be authentic and transparent in your social media communications.

Internal Investigations: When to Dig Deep, When to Bring in Outside Counsel

Deciding When an Internal Investigation Is Necessary. Not every internal issue requires a formal investigation. But some do. A well-designed internal investigation can help a company identify and address potential problems before they escalate into legal or reputational crises.

Regulatory Enforcement. Is there a risk of regulatory enforcement? If yes, investigate.

Financial Statements. Could it impact financial statements or SEC filings? If yes, investigate.

Senior Leadership. Does it involve senior leadership? If yes, bring in outside counsel.

Criminal Liability. Is there potential criminal liability? If yes, bring in outside counsel.

Seriousness of the Allegation. The more serious the allegation, the more likely it is that an investigation is necessary.

Credibility of the Source. The more credible the source of the allegation, the more likely it is that an investigation is necessary.

Potential for Legal or Reputational Harm. The greater the potential for legal or reputational harm, the more likely it is that an investigation is necessary.

Company Culture. A company with a strong culture of compliance is more likely to conduct internal investigations than a company with a weak culture of compliance.

Running an Internal Investigation the Right Way

Define the Scope. Clearly define the scope of the investigation. What specific allegations are you investigating? Who needs to be involved? What evidence needs to be collected? A well-defined scope will help you focus your resources and avoid wasting time on irrelevant issues.

Document Everything (But Be Careful). Assume regulators and courts will see your notes. Stick to factual findings—no speculation or opinions in emails. Maintain a detailed record of all steps taken during the investigation, including interviews, document reviews, and expert consultations.

Deliver a Clear Action Plan. If misconduct is found, disciplinary actions must be swift and fair. If regulatory reporting is required, control the messaging and disclosures. Develop a plan for remediating the underlying issues that led to the misconduct and preventing similar incidents from occurring in the future.

Choose an Appropriate Investigator. Select an investigator with the appropriate skills and experience for the matter at hand.

Develop an Investigation Plan. Develop a detailed investigation plan that outlines the steps to be taken during the investigation.

Conduct Interviews. Conduct thorough and well-documented interviews of all relevant witnesses.

Gather and Review Documents. Gather and review all relevant documents and electronic data.

Analyze the Evidence. Analyze the evidence to determine whether there is sufficient evidence to support the allegations.
Prepare a Report. Prepare a written report that summarizes the findings of the investigation and makes recommendations for corrective action.
Implement Corrective Action. Implement corrective action to address the underlying issues that led to the misconduct.
Monitor Compliance. Monitor compliance with the corrective action plan to ensure that the misconduct does not recur.

Building a Crisis-Resilient Culture

Beyond reacting to crises, the best GCs proactively build a crisis-resilient culture within their organizations. This involves embedding ethical values, promoting open communication, and fostering a sense of accountability at all levels of the company.

Ethical Leadership. Set the tone from the top. Ensure that senior leaders are committed to ethical behavior and compliance with all applicable laws and regulations.
Open Communication. Encourage employees to speak up about potential problems without fear of retaliation. Create channels for employees to report concerns anonymously.
Training and Education. Provide regular training to employees on ethical conduct, compliance policies, and crisis management procedures.
Risk Assessments. Conduct regular risk assessments to identify potential vulnerabilities and develop strategies for mitigating those risks.
Scenario Planning. Conduct scenario planning exercises to prepare for potential crises.
Regular Drills. Conduct regular drills to test the effectiveness of the company's crisis management plan.
Continuous Improvement. Continuously review and improve the company's crisis management plan based on lessons learned from past experiences.

Five-Point Framework for Crisis Mode

1. Stabilize Fast, Lead Calmly

Control the Narrative. Collaborate immediately with PR to issue fact-based, legally vetted messaging. Get ahead of leaks and misinformation.

Form a Unified Response Team. Legal, PR, HR, IT, Compliance—working in lockstep from Day One.

Reassure Internally. Address employee concerns, shut down speculation, and keep communication disciplined.

GC Mindset—Be the calmest person in the room. Speed and clarity win the first 48 hours.

2. Contain the Legal and Reputational Fallout

Preserve Evidence. Issue legal holds, work with IT, and monitor compliance. Spoliation is a crisis multiplier.

Assess Exposure. Identify potential litigation, regulatory triggers, and disclosure obligations. Engage outside counsel early.

Control Communications. Everything internal is discoverable. One rogue email or off-the-cuff comment can set you back months.

GC Mantra—If it's written down, assume it will be Exhibit A.

3. Investigate Decisively: but Strategically

Decide Scope and Method. Not every issue needs outside counsel, but serious, complex, or senior-level issues do.

Maintain Privilege. Structure investigations through counsel, document carefully, and avoid speculation in writing.

Deliver Action. If wrongdoing is found, take corrective steps fast—discipline, remediation, disclosure, and prevention.

GC Skillset—Combine investigative rigor with judgment. You're not just a lawyer; you do triage, are a truth finder, and a diplomat.

4. Communicate with Precision and Empathy

Say Something Before Someone Else Does. Delay equals distrust. Silence implies guilt.

Craft Every Word. Work with PR to ensure messaging is transparent, consistent, and doesn't create legal exposure.

Manage Social Media. Monitor, correct misinformation, and keep executives away from the "post" button.

GC Rule—Every message must work for regulators, shareholders, employees, and the court of public opinion.

5. Protect the Culture: and the Whistleblowers

Zero Tolerance for Retaliation. Retaliation turns a molehill into a mountain of regulatory pain.

Encourage Reporting, Not Fear. Promote anonymous reporting channels and respond to complaints with seriousness and documentation.

Build a Resilient Culture. Crises are a stress test of values. Ethical leadership, trust, and preparation must already be in place.

GC Legacy—How you treat the truth-tellers will define how your company is remembered, and how regulators respond.

Case Studies

Scenario I: The Overlooked Complaint That Became a Front-Page Headline

At ApexMed, a mid-sized healthcare technology company, a junior compliance analyst submitted an internal complaint alleging that a sales manager was pushing clients to buy diagnostic software using exaggerated claims of FDA approval. The general counsel's office quickly dismissed it as a misunderstanding. After all, the manager in question was a top performer, and the complaint came from someone perceived as inexperienced and difficult.

No formal investigation was conducted. No documentation. No interview with the complainant. The email was quietly marked "closed."

Three months later, the same analyst, frustrated and feeling ignored, forwarded the complaint to a reporter at a healthcare watchdog publication. Within days, the story broke online under the headline, *Whistleblower Alleges Misleading Sales Tactics at ApexMed.*

The article went viral.

The FDA opened an inquiry. The company's stock dropped 18% in two days. Plaintiffs' firms began advertising potential class actions. Worse, when regulators requested ApexMed's internal investigation file, all they received was an email with a single sentence, "This claim appears meritless."

- Because the complaint hadn't been taken seriously at the start:
- There was no clear paper trail to show any genuine effort to assess the claim.
- There was no protection of the whistleblower's identity—now revealed by press speculation—leading to internal chatter and fears of retaliation.
- There was no documentation to support the company's assertion that it acted in good faith.

Had ApexMed acknowledged the complaint, interviewed key parties, and documented its findings, even to conclude that the claim lacked merit, it would've had a defensible process. Instead, the optics suggested indifference, and that perception became the company's reality.

Key Takeaway

Even complaints that seem flimsy deserve a measured, professional response. If you think no one will ever see your handling of a complaint, assume regulators, journalists, and opposing counsel eventually will.

Scenario II: The Sales Director's Complaint and the Lesson in Retaliation

A regional sales director at a publicly traded manufacturing company submitted an internal whistleblower report alleging that a senior VP had directed teams to falsify quarterly sales figures to meet earnings targets. The sales director, Lauren, submitted the report anonymously via the company's ethics hotline. The compliance team quickly began a preliminary assessment and flagged the complaint as credible.

Misstep

Within two weeks, word quietly spread that Lauren was the likely whistleblower. Although no formal announcement was made, her name surfaced during internal meetings, and some colleagues began distancing themselves from her. Her manager, who was close to the accused VP, reassigned Lauren to a less strategic territory, cutting her potential commissions by 40% and removing her from a high-profile client pitch. Soon after, she was excluded from leadership calls and skipped over for a promotion she had been promised.

Escalation

Lauren, feeling isolated and professionally sidelined, retained counsel and filed a complaint with the SEC and OSHA under the Sarbanes-Oxley Act, alleging retaliation. The company's failure to protect her identity and prevent workplace retaliation triggered a broader regulatory investigation, not just into the accounting practices but also into the company's compliance culture. The SEC began scrutinizing the company's whistleblower procedures, while media outlets picked up the story, linking it to corporate governance failures.

Response and Lessons Reinforced

The legal and compliance teams, now on the defensive, implemented an emergency remediation plan and:
- publicly reaffirmed the company's anti-retaliation policy
- removed the manager who had reassigned Lauren
- instituted mandatory anti-retaliation training for all executives and front-line managers
- established a monitoring protocol to audit whistleblower treatment post-reporting
- created a cross-functional whistleblower response team with Legal, HR, and Compliance oversight

Key Takeaways
- Any adverse action—perceived or real—against a whistleblower is a legal and reputational landmine.
- Confidentiality must be airtight. Even "unofficial leaks" of identity undermine trust and trigger liability.
- Training and monitoring are not "nice to have"—they are guardrails against escalation.
- Retaliation doesn't just hurt the whistleblower; it can bring down the house.

This scenario underscores the importance of embedding a zero-tolerance, prevention-first mindset for retaliation into the corporate DNA, before the first complaint ever lands.

Scenario III: Assessing Legal Exposure After a Misleading Investor Call

TechNova Inc., a publicly traded software company, recently held its quarterly earnings call. During the call, the CEO stated that a major contract with a federal agency had been finalized and would significantly boost Q4 revenues. The company's stock jumped 12% in two days.

Two weeks later, a whistleblower from the sales team contacted the general counsel, disclosing that the contract in question had not been signed. In fact, negotiations had stalled over compliance concerns, and the deal was unlikely to close in the near term.

What Happens Next

Identifying Legal Claims

The general counsel immediately convenes a crisis legal team, including securities specialists and outside counsel. Together, they identify several areas of legal exposure:

Securities fraud. The CEO's statements may have misled investors and artificially inflated the stock price.

Regulatory Violations. Potential violation of SEC disclosure rules.

Employment Violations. Possible retaliation risk if the whistleblower is not protected.

Evaluating Litigation and Regulatory Risk

The legal team assesses that the misleading statements could lead to:

- shareholder class actions
- an SEC investigation into material misstatements
- DOJ scrutiny, depending on whether intent can be established

The team quantifies the potential exposure in dollars, reputational damage, and disruption to leadership.

Preparing for Government Inquiries

Anticipating SEC involvement, the team begins assembling all relevant emails, board materials, and internal communications related to the contract. They also identify key individuals to be interviewed and prepare them for possible regulatory interviews.

Engaging Outside Counsel

The company retains a top securities litigation firm with experience handling high-profile SEC investigations. The outside firm immediately helps implement a document hold, communicates with the SEC on a no-fault basis, and advises on disclosure strategy.

Conducting an Internal Investigation
An independent internal investigation reveals that the CEO exaggerated the deal's status based on a verbal assurance from the agency, without consulting legal or sales leadership. This finding shapes the company's eventual disclosure and defense strategy.

Assessing Insurance Coverage
The company's risk management team and outside insurance counsel review D&O insurance and errors & omissions policies. Fortunately, the policies cover defense costs and settlement liability up to $25 million, giving the company a financial buffer.

Key Takeaway
By moving quickly to assess legal exposure across multiple dimensions—litigation, regulatory, employment, and financial—TechNova contains the damage, avoids compounding errors, and puts itself in the best position to respond strategically. The early engagement of outside counsel and preparation for regulatory scrutiny make all the difference in managing the fallout.

Scenario IV: The Data Breach at Velonix Inc.

Velonix Inc., a publicly traded healthcare technology company, discovers a significant data breach affecting over 300,000 patient records. The breach was caused by a vulnerability in a third-party vendor's software. The company's legal and PR teams are notified late on a Friday afternoon.

What Went Right—and Why It Mattered

Immediate Coordination

The GC convenes an emergency meeting that night with PR, IT, compliance, and the CEO. Together, they create a unified response plan. The GC insists on reviewing all public statements before release, knowing that legal and reputational exposure are now intertwined.

Transparent and Timely Messaging. By Saturday morning, Velonix issues a short but clear statement acknowledging the breach, confirming it's under investigation, and assuring that patient care systems remain unaffected. They avoid spin, stick to known facts, and commit to regular updates.

Control of the Narrative. Rather than waiting for media leaks, Velonix contacts key journalists and regulators first. This preempts speculation and ensures the company's framing of the facts leads the coverage. Internal messaging mirrors the external message to ensure consistency and reduce employee confusion.

Tone: Empathetic and Responsible. The CEO issues a video statement by Sunday evening: *We sincerely apologize to the patients whose information was compromised. This should not have happened. We're investigating fully, strengthening our systems, and offering identity protection to all affected. We own this, and we will fix it.*

The tone is empathetic, direct, and devoid of legalese. It's reviewed line-by-line by the GC and PR to avoid any admissions of liability while still taking responsibility.

Prepared for Leaks. Sure enough, by Monday, an internal email chain speculating on vendor liability leaks to a tech blog. But because Velonix's public narrative is already established, the leak gains little traction. The leaked messages, while pointed, are professional thanks to prior guidance from Legal to write every internal email as if it could end up in *The New York Times*.

Outcome

Despite the seriousness of the breach, Velonix's stock price dips only modestly and rebounds within two weeks. Regulators commend the company's cooperation. Plaintiffs' lawyers still file lawsuits, but the well-documented, transparent response limits claims of gross negligence. The PR nightmare is avoided, not because the crisis didn't happen, but because it was managed correctly from the first moment.

This scenario reinforces the central lessons:

- Legal and PR must move as one.
- Fast, honest, coordinated communication beats defensiveness or delay.
- Empathy and responsibility are not liabilities; they're shields.
- The real crisis is not the breach; it's how you respond.

Scenario V: Anonymous Tip About Revenue Recognition Triggers Full-Scale Investigation

On a quiet Monday morning in Q1, the company's whistleblower hotline receives an anonymous report stating that "senior sales leadership in the Western Region" is backdating software license agreements to pull future revenue into Q4 to meet year-end earnings targets. The tip is detailed—it names a regional VP of Sales, references specific customer deals, and claims that the CFO "was aware" of the behavior and signed off on it.

Initial Response: "Deciding Whether to Investigate"

The General Counsel (GC) immediately convenes a triage meeting with the Chief Compliance Officer, Chief Internal Auditor, and Head of HR. They evaluate the tip against the following investigation criteria.

Regulatory Enforcement Risk. The behavior implicates revenue recognition—a hot-button issue for the SEC. Check.

SEC Filing Impact. Inflated Q4 earnings would mislead investors and require a restatement. Check.

Involves Senior Leadership. The CFO is allegedly involved. That alone demands outside counsel. Check.

Criminal Liability. If true, the conduct could constitute securities fraud. Check.

Credibility of the Source. The whistleblower provides specific names, deal references, and timing. Credible. Check.

Reputational Risk. A public accounting scandal could crush investor confidence. Check.

Verdict

A full investigation is needed, and it can't be handled internally.

Escalation – "Bring in Outside Counsel"

The GC immediately contacts a white-collar defense firm with SEC experience and retains a forensic accounting firm. This checks several boxes by:

- ensuring objectivity and independence
- signaling to regulators and the Audit Committee that the company is taking the issue seriously
- protecting attorney-client privilege and work product by channeling findings through outside counsel
- bringing in the technical accounting expertise necessary to evaluate complex revenue recognition rules under ASC 606

Outside counsel helps draft the investigation charter, defines the scope, and interviews key stakeholders, including the whistleblower (whose anonymity is preserved), regional finance leads, and senior sales executives.

Investigation Phase: "Running an Internal Investigation the Right Way"

1. Define the Scope.
The investigation focuses on software license contracts from Q3 and Q4, involving the Western Region, and the involvement of the CFO, controller, and regional sales leads. Outside counsel defines a two-month lookback window and asks forensic accountants to examine the contract metadata, including timestamps, email threads, and DocuSign logs.

2. Preserve Evidence.
A legal hold is issued to 45 employees. IT suspends all automated email and chat deletions and preserves backup systems. Communications explicitly warn employees not to "clean up" files. Compliance and legal teams monitor hold compliance weekly.

3. Conduct Interviews.
Counsel conducts 20+ interviews with counsel present and prepares summaries with only factual findings—no speculation or editorializing. Special care is taken when interviewing employees who report to implicated executives to avoid chilling effects or coercion.

4. Review Documents.
The forensic accounting team reviews hundreds of contracts and finds ten deals that were backdated, with email chains suggesting deliberate manipulation. In several of them, legal and finance teams had raised concerns that were overridden by senior sales executives.

5. Analyze the Evidence.
Outside counsel prepares a matrix comparing booking dates, contract execution dates, and revenue recognition entries. The team identifies a pattern that aligns with quarterly sales targets and board pressure to "hit the number."

6. Document Everything (Carefully).
All notes, memos, and findings are stored in a secure, privilege-protected folder. Outside counsel repeatedly reminds the investigation team to stick to facts in all written communication—no guessing, no speculation, and no inflammatory language.

7. Reporting.
Counsel presents findings to the Audit Committee in a written report. The findings confirm intentional backdating by the regional VP, with knowledge of the Western SVP. The CFO failed to act on red flags but didn't directly participate. The report avoids conclusions about criminal intent and instead frames findings around fact patterns, policy violations, and GAAP inconsistencies.

Remediation and Follow-Up: "Deliver a Clear Action Plan"
Discipline. The regional VP and SVP of Sales are terminated. The CFO receives a written reprimand and is replaced six months later, following a broader leadership shakeup.
Disclosure. The company files an 8-K disclosing that it will restate Q4 results and has launched a remediation plan. The restatement reduces earnings by 8%.
Training. A new company-wide training program is launched on revenue recognition policies and ethical reporting.
Policy Changes.
- Deal review protocols now require dual sign-off from Legal and Finance.
- Incentive comp is adjusted to reduce pressure on quarter-end sales. The Audit Committee now receives quarterly compliance heat maps.

8. Monitor Compliance.
Internal Audit is tasked with ongoing monitoring of contract booking practices. The company performs random sampling of contracts quarterly. New analytics dashboards flag date discrepancies in real time.

Result
While the financial restatement causes a short-term dip in stock price, the company's decisive action and transparency are well-received by investors. The SEC opens an inquiry but declines to pursue formal enforcement due to the company's voluntary disclosure, cooperation, and remedial

actions. Internally, employee trust improves, especially after leadership communicates that integrity matters more than "making the quarter."

Final Thought: Be Ready Before the Crisis Hits

Every company will face a crisis. The ones that survive—and even thrive—are those that respond swiftly, strategically, and ethically. Your role as GC isn't just to clean up the mess; it's to prevent it from becoming a catastrophe. A crisis is not just a threat; it's also an opportunity to demonstrate leadership, build trust, and strengthen the company's culture.

So, the real question is, are you ready? Have you prepared your team, your company, and yourself for the inevitable challenges that lie ahead? The answer to this question will determine your success as a General Counsel and the long-term viability of your organization.

Conclusion

Remember that 8:31 a.m. call from the GC at ACME? The company with the maintenance test failure that threatened the lives of hundreds of people. A failure exposed in print by an investment-bank analyst.

Let me tell you exactly what we did to save the day. We moved fast. Not recklessly. Not emotionally. But deliberately, and in parallel. Within minutes, we deployed a coordinated, four-part response designed to do one thing: stop the bleeding before panic hardened into fact.

First, We Confronted the False Narrative Head-On

The General Counsel sent a cease-and-desist letter to the investment bank—immediate, precise, and unforgiving. It laid out, in detail, every scientific and technical flaw in the analyst's report. It demanded withdrawal. And it made clear, without theatrics but without apology, that the company was prepared to litigate.

Silence, in moments like this, is consent. Legal pressure changes the dynamics instantly. It tells the market—and the analyst—that this company is not confused, not hiding, and not afraid to push back.

Next, We Put Credibility on Air

GC leveraged one of the company's directors, who was a former regulator—someone the market trusted and the media recognized. We got him on cable news immediately. No speculation. No spin. Just a calm, authoritative explanation of why the maintenance could not have caused the failure being alleged.

The effect was immediate. In minutes, not days, the story shifted from "company at fault" to "facts still emerging." That distinction matters. In a crisis, buying credibility is often more valuable than buying time.

At the Same Time, We Stopped the Market Damage

GC asked the CFO to request a trading halt under the New York Exchange Rules, citing false information materially impacting the stock price. It was the right call—and the hard one. Halts are scrutinized. But leadership under pressure often is. The halt did three things at once: it prevented further erosion, signaled confidence, and created breathing room to correct the record before speculation calcified into valuation.

Finally, Before Trading Resumed, We Reassured Those Who Mattered Most

The GC worked with Investor Relations to get the CEO and CFO directly into a meeting with top investors, walking them through the facts in plain language. No hedging. No legalese. Just the truth, clearly explained. Then the company issued an 8-K, putting accurate information into the market for everyone at the same time. That closed the loop. It eliminated the information vacuum. And it restored trust.

By the close of that day's trading, the results spoke for themselves.
- The research note was withdrawn.
- The stock recovered all its losses and finished the day up.
- Investors were reassured.
- The board exhaled.

And the General Counsel—the person everyone had been staring at when the floor dropped out—emerged not as a back-office advisor, but as the leader who held the company together when it mattered most.

A crisis that could have metastasized into years of litigation, regulatory scrutiny, and lost value was contained—and reversed—in hours.

That's the job. Not knowing the law in the abstract. Not waiting for perfect information, but understanding how power, credibility, timing, and judgment intersect when the clock is running, and the margin for error is zero.

This job is not for spectators. If you want comfort, predictability, and clean lines between "legal" and "business," there are plenty of other roles where the lights are dimmer and the consequences are smaller. The public company General Counsel's role is different. It is louder. Faster. Less forgiving.

And it is one of the most consequential seats in the enterprise. You sit at the intersection of risk and reality. When things are calm, you help steer strategy. When things break, you become the last line of defense between chaos and control. There is no pause button. No second draft. No one else is coming through the door to save the day.

That responsibility is not a burden. It is a mandate.

The best General Counsels don't wait to be invited into the conversation. They don't hide behind memos or hedge when clarity is required. They understand the business as deeply as the CEO, the numbers as fluently as the CFO, and the psychology of the boardroom as well as anyone in it. They act early. They speak plainly. And when the moment comes, they lead.

This Book is Not About Being Perfect

It's about being *prepared:*
  - to make decisions with incomplete information
  - to challenge bad assumptions, even when they come from powerful voices
  - to move faster than the market, the media, and sometimes your own fear

You will not always be popular. You will not always be thanked. But if you do this job right, there will be moments—quiet ones, often invisible to the outside world—when a company survives, stabilizes, or succeeds because you knew what mattered and acted when it counted.

Those moments define careers. They define legacies. So don't wait for the crisis to figure out who you are in it.
- Build the muscle now.
- Learn the business.
- Earn the trust.
- Claim the seat.

Because someday—maybe tomorrow—your phone will light up at 8:31 a.m. And when it does, the company will be looking to you.

Make sure you're ready to answer.

Index

Business acumen (see Financial and
Business Acumen)
Buybacks (see Share buybacks)
Bylaws
  advance notice provisions, 201
  staggered boards, 201, 217-219
  supermajority voting requirements,
201-202

C

Capital allocation
  buybacks (see Share buybacks)
  dividends, 143, 151
  free cash flow and, 143-145
  legal risk in, 151
Capital expenditures (CapEx), 143
Cash flow statement
  financing activities, 143
  investing activities, 143
  operating activities, 142-143
  overview for GCs, 142-144
CEO
  balancing legal risk with vision, 26-28
  communicating legal advice to, 27-28
  managing relationship with GC,
26-28
  risk appetite, 26
  strategic vision of, 26-27
CFO
  cost control focus, 25
  financial stewardship, 25
  GC relationship with, 25, 28-29,
160-161
  regulatory compliance focus, 25
  risk management approach, 25
CCPA (California Consumer Privacy
Act), 21, 129
CHRO (Chief Human Resources
Officer) (Chapter 3), 49-74
  cultural landmines, 15, 49
  strategic partnering for people,
culture, and compliance, 50
Clawback policies, 156

Class action lawsuits
  disclosure failures and, 162-163, 193-
195
  EPS manipulation and, 162-163
  securities fraud claims, 147,149, 150,
154, 192–195
Classified board (see Staggered board)
Communication skills
  earnings calls, 181-188, 194-196
  executive communication, 18-19,
27-29
  translating legal concepts, 29-30
Compliance
  compliance as business priority, 196
  compliance training, 17, 196
  culture of compliance, 17, 187-188,
196
  global regulations, 17
Conscience of the company (GC role),
4, 20-22
Contract disputes
  in-house lawyer case study, 132-135
  negotiation tactics, 132-135
  supplier renegotiation, 132-135
Corporate governance
  boardroom best practices, 75-103,
199–225
  GC's role in, 17-22, 199–225
  governance framework, 201-202,
211–213
  governance roadshows, 202, 212,
217-219
  (see also Board of Directors)
Corporate scandals
  handling, 231-240
  whistleblower claims, 236-238
  (see also Crisis Mode)
Cost of goods sold (COGS), 140
Credibility
  building with board, 75-103
  building with CEO and CFO, 24-47
Crisis management (Chapter 9), 227-
258